© 2019 Lifeway Press

Reprinted May 2023

Josh Hayes, Chris Johnson, Brett McIntosh, Reid Patton,
Tyler Quillet, Rob Tims, Amber Vaden
Writers

Chris Johnson, Amber Vaden
Content Editors

Dawn Woods
Production Editor

Darin Clark
Art Director/Designer

Tyler Quillet
Editorial Team Lead

John Paul Basham
Director, Adult Ministries

Ben Mandrell
President, Lifeway Christian Resources

Published by © 2019 Lifeway Press®
Reprinted July 2022

ISBN 978-1-0877-0308-4 • Item 005824188

Dewey decimal classification: 248.84
Subject headings: CHRISTIAN LIFE / DISCIPLESHIP

We believe that the Bible has God for its author; salvation for its
end; and truth, without any mixture of error, for its matter and that
all Scripture is totally true and trustworthy. To review Lifeway's
doctrinal guideline, please visit lifeway.com/doctrinalguideline.

To order additional copies of this resource, write to:
Lifeway Resources Customer Service;
200 Powell Place, Suite 100; Brentwood, TN 37027-7707; fax 615-251-
5933; call toll free 800-458-2772; order online at Lifeway.com;
or email orderentry@lifeway.com.

Printed in the United States of America

Groups Ministry Publishing, Lifeway Resources
200 Powell Place, Suite 100, Brentwood, TN 37027-7707

My New Life

. . .

A New Christian's Guide to Building Your Life on God's Word

NAME:

_____

Getting Started in the Christian Life

Lifeway Press® • *Brentwood, TN*

SO IF YOU HAVE BEEN RAISED WITH CHRIST, SEEK THE THINGS ABOVE,

WHERE CHRIST IS, SEATED AT THE RIGHT HAND OF GOD. SET YOUR MINDS

ON THINGS ABOVE, NOT ON EARTHLY THINGS. COLOSSIANS 3:1-2

Table of Contents

Introduction

Welcome to *My New Life: A New Christian's Guide to Building Your Life on God's Word*! The Bible tells us there is incredible joy and celebration in heaven when someone chooses to place their trust in Jesus Christ (Luke 15:7,10). We, too, celebrate this step of faith with you. This is an exciting time for you, but also a time that you might question, "Now what?"

As you begin this journey of trusting Jesus, our desire is to give you foundational truths from God's Word that you will stand on for the rest of your life. May your faith in God and understanding of His Word deepen as you seek Him through these pages. Welcome to the family of God!

IT'S ALL ABOUT GOD

So, now you are a Christian, but what does that *really* mean? As you'll read in the coming pages, it is all about God, His great love for you, and your continued response of trust in Him.

> **"But God, who is rich in mercy, because of his great love that he had for us, made us alive with Christ even though we were dead in trespasses. You are saved by grace!"** (Ephesians 2:4-5).

God is so gracious that He sent His One and only Son, Jesus, to make us right with Him. We were once without hope and God graciously offered hope through His Son. This generous gift wasn't given because of anything we have done, but by what He has done for us!

> **"God's love was revealed among us in this way: God sent his one and only Son into the world so that we might live through him"** (1 John 4:9).

The good news is that Christ died for your sins, was buried, and was raised from the dead. This is the gospel, the foundation of our faith. The word *gospel* means "good news."

> **"For I passed on to you as most important what I also received: that Christ died for our sins according to the Scriptures, that he was buried, that he was raised on the third day according to the Scriptures"** (1 Corinthians 15:3-4).

You have responded to God's love by accepting Jesus as your personal Lord and Savior. By doing so, you have been saved and are promised eternal life with Him!

> **"If you confess with your mouth, 'Jesus is Lord,' and believe in your heart that God raised him from the dead, you will be saved"** (Romans 10:9).

Today, Jesus is alive and at work in your life! So what are the implications of this? What does it mean now that you've chosen to trust Him with your life? What does this mean for you moving forward?

These are just a few of the questions we want to help you answer in the pages ahead.

GOD INITIATES, WE RESPOND

"We love because he first loved us" (1 John 4:19). It all starts with God loving us. God initiates a relationship with us and we respond by believing in Him. God desires for this to be a continuing, ongoing relationship. In this study, you will discover some basics of how a relationship with God works. It begins with coming to know God through His Word, the Bible. God tells us about Himself and what He expects of us through the written Word of God. He actually speaks to us through His Word. We respond by reading the Bible, understanding it, and obeying His teachings. We learn to do what His Word says. James 1:22 instructs us to "be doers of the word and not hearers only." James goes on to say, "the one who looks intently into the perfect law of freedom and perseveres in it, and is not a forgetful hearer but a doer who works — this person will be blessed in what he does" (James 1:25).

Throughout this book, we'll hear from God's Word and this resource will help you respond to Him. It will show you how to personally begin to live your daily life in Christ. This is likely new for you, but we promise not to overwhelm you with too much information, and you have the freedom to go at your own pace. You'll take tiny bites of truth each day, which will train and guide you as you make God's word your foundation.

How did you become aware of your need to become a Christian?

_____

_____

_____

When did you acknowledge your need for Jesus? Describe what that was like.

_____

_____

_____

Who was influential in sharing the good news of God's love with you?

_____

_____

_____

•   •   •

What to Expect from This Resource

BIBLE READING AND PRAYER

The Bible is God's message to us. Since He is the God of all truth, we can trust that His teachings are completely reliable.

- The Bible was inspired by the Holy Spirit and written by men.

- The Bible is completely without error; it is holy.

- The Bible, also known as God's Word, is our trustworthy source for guidance from God. In its pages, we will learn about God and get wise instructions for following Him.

One of the benefits of being a follower of Christ is prayer. Prayer gives us 24/7 access to God. Because we are His children, He invites us to talk to Him, approaching Him as a loving Father. As you read God's Word and go about your everyday life, respond to Him in prayer.

WHAT'S AHEAD?

Each day, you will read Scripture passages related to that day's topic. You'll also find questions that will help you respond to God. The day's study will end with a prayer focus. We encourage you to begin hiding God's Word in your heart by memorizing Scripture. You'll find a memory verse or verses on the opening page of each week (see page 10 for an example). Post this somewhere you'll see often, read it daily (break it down into smaller sections, if necessary), or repeat it aloud throughout the week until you have it memorized.

You'll gain a deeper understanding at a heart level about what the gospel is, who God is, what your life in Christ looks like, the value of belonging to a church, and God's mission for you. Although you will gain a lot of knowledge, which is a good thing, our hope is that there would be true heart transformation as you grow as a disciple of Jesus Christ. This resource will help you build a foundation for your faith, but this resource does not take the place of the Bible. We'll give you the foundation to help you grow, but you need to also spend time in God's Word and in prayer, seeking Him.

We hope you have someone to do this alongside you. It's most helpful if this person has been following Jesus for some time so they can answer your questions. If you go through this alone, that is OK, too. But if you desire someone who trusts and loves Jesus to walk with you through this book, please ask this individual. If you don't know of anyone, ask your pastor to connect you with someone.

This book is just the beginning of your journey to discovering life in Jesus. We trust that the ensuing pages will give you a longing to dig deeper into God's Word.

How to Use This Resource

First, you'll need a Bible. Don't have one? Find one here: **LifeWay.com/Bibles.** In this resource, we will use the Christian Standard Bible.

· · ·

Each day has a Bible verse, a short explanation of the verse and main idea, questions for you to ponder and respond to, and a guide to help you pray. Take your time as you ponder these truths of God's Word and be intentional to respond to God as you go.

· · ·

At the end of each week, you will find additional journaling pages. Use this space to reflect on the truths you are learning, how God is changing your heart, and what you will do with what you have learned.

· · ·

You can work through this book individually or with another mature Christian. If you work through it on your own, be sure to write down questions in the notes section that you feel you may need to ask other, mature believers.

· · ·

Take the time you need. Don't feel rushed to get it done. Soak in the truths of God's Word at your own pace.

My New Life in Christ

Therefore, if anyone is in Christ, he is a new creation; the old has passed away, and see, the new has come!

2 CORINTHIANS 5:17

MAIN IDEA:

When you become a follower of Jesus, He makes everything new. Since you believe in Jesus, you are now different and your life will begin to look different. Fortunately, the Bible helps us know how to become a Christian and it also gives us guidance about how to embrace this new life. This first session offers basic instruction for living the Christian life.

WEEK *1*

MY NEW LIFE

Your New Life

TODAY'S TRUTH: When you become a Christian you are saved by grace and made alive in Christ.

MAIN SCRIPTURE: Ephesians 2:4-5

"Dead men do not bleed."

That's what the doctor told his patient.

This patient was special; his family admitted him because he kept insisting he was dead. Not merely in an emotional or figurative sense, but dead in a clinical, biological sense. The doctor attempted to reason with this incredulous patient, pointing out to him that dead people do not breathe, walk, or talk as he was doing. These observations did not seem relevant to the man.

Since the man persisted in the belief that he was dead, the doctor pulled out some medical textbooks in order to show him the typical characteristics of an expired human corpse, one of them being that dead bodies do not bleed when they are punctured. The patient at last looked as if he might change his mind, nodding his head and stating, "That's right. Dead men don't bleed." To demonstrate to the man indisputably that he was not dead, the doctor poked his finger with a needle. The man's finger bled. The patient then looked at the doctor and exclaimed, "Wow! Dead men do bleed after all!"

This humorous story about a man's belief that he was dead might seem preposterous, but the statement "we were dead in trespasses" (Ephesians 2:5) might also sound ridiculous to us. Nonetheless, this is what the Bible teaches is true about us before we were saved. Because of "sin"—which is anything we think, say, or do that opposes God—the Bible describes our condition as "dead in trespasses" (Ephesians 2:5). We weren't dead in a physical sense, but we were spiritually dead. With respect to our relationship with God, we were dead men and women walking.

When did you first begin to recognize sin in your own life?
How did you respond to this?

_____

_____

_____

Before Christ's forgiveness, we were sinners who followed our own selfish desires. We *were* subject to death and condemnation. But not anymore! The key word in the previous sentences is the past tense verb "were." No longer are those things true of us if we belong to Jesus, having placed our full trust in Him for salvation and committing to turn away from a life of sin.

We were dead until God saved us by His grace. The Bible states, "God, who is rich in mercy, because of his great love that he had for us, made us alive with Christ" (Ephesians 2:4-5). If we believe in Jesus, then we are made alive with Him. In a real sense, before we trusted in Jesus for salvation, we were only breathing corpses. Now, since we belong to Him who died and was raised, we are truly alive, capable of following the good ways of God instead of the evil ways of this world. No longer dead, we are, as the Bible states elsewhere, "a new creation" in Christ; old, dead things have passed away (2 Corinthians 5:17).

How does it make you feel to know that Jesus is able to forgive your sins?

_____

_____

_____

We were dead, and dead people cannot help themselves. This is part of the reason the Bible emphasizes we "are saved by grace" (Ephesians 2:5). The word _grace_ refers to our receiving God's favor even though we have done nothing to deserve it; in fact, we have done everything opposite of deserving it. Grace is God's unmerited blessing. We were spiritually dead and incapable of doing anything to commend ourselves to God. By grace alone, apart from any good we have done, is how we are made alive with Christ.

Though we freely receive this saving grace, it came at the greatest of costs—the death and resurrection of God's Son, Jesus. Because of God's love toward us in Jesus, spiritually dead men and women can be made alive.

PRAYER: Father, thank You for making me alive in Your Son, Jesus. Without Your grace, I would still be dead in my trespasses and blindly traveling down the path of sin. Because of what You have revealed in the Bible, I now have a better understanding of who I was before I met Jesus and of who I am eternally in Him. I praise You for the richness of Your love and mercy. Help me to continue learning what it means to be alive in Christ. In Jesus' name, I pray, Amen.

NOTES

_____

_____

_____

_____

. . .

Enjoy God's Presence

TODAY'S TRUTH: God's call to remain in Him is an invitation to experience His presence in our daily lives.

MAIN SCRIPTURE: John 15:1-5

Imagine that you are just a few days away from taking the vacation of a lifetime. For weeks, if not months, you will be traveling the world and taking in all of its wonders. While you would obviously be very excited about your trip, there would be many things to do before you leave. What will you do with your pets? And what about the mail? Your bills? How will you acquire the different currencies you need for different countries? Do you need visas, or is a passport sufficient? The list of things you might need to do to enjoy your vacation can quickly overwhelm you and dampen your enthusiasm for the trip.

Similarly, while becoming a Christian is very exciting, it can quickly become overwhelming and even dampen your enthusiasm for your faith. One moment you are joyously celebrating what God has done in your life, and the next you are overwhelmed with all the things you are supposed to "do" to grow as a Christian.

Jesus' simple words from John 15:4-5 bring us great comfort. Read them carefully:

"Remain in me, and I in you. Just as a branch is unable to produce fruit by itself unless it remains on the vine, neither can you unless you remain in me. I am the vine; you are the branches. The one who remains in me and I in him produces much fruit, because you can do nothing without me."

What do you find encouraging in these verses?

_____

_____

_____

What do you find challenging about Jesus' command to "remain" in Him?

_____

_____

_____

These words bring an enormous amount of clarity and simplicity to new believers fretting about how to be a Christian. Jesus simply says: "Remain in me" (John 15:4). Some Bible translations use the word "abide." What Jesus is saying is "stick with Me" or "stay connected to Me."

In the Gospel of John, Jesus frequently uses the word "remain." When Jesus invited His disciples to remain in Him, He meant for them to walk with Him, and continually pursue and obey Him. To our ears this might seem like a duty or chore, but Jesus assures us that if we remain in Him, we will find our greatest joy in being connected to God through Him. Pursuing and obeying Jesus is not a duty, but a delight.

This raises two very important questions: First, how does one "remain" in Jesus? You will learn more about this as you continue through this book, but for now it's enough to understand that "remaining" is as simple as talking to God in prayer and listening to His word as you read the Bible with His people, the church. The "fruit" that comes of that is godly behavior—loving God and loving others as He has loved you.

Second, what is "fruit"? Fruit is what Jesus wants to produce in you. If you will remain in Jesus, then He will make you more and more into the person He called you to be. Jesus can transform you to become just like Him. Jesus' instruction to His followers is that they must be constantly reliant upon Him in order to become more and more like Him.

Read the following prayer and try to pray to God using your own words as you feel comfortable.

PRAYER: Father, I humbly ask that You keep me close to Jesus through regular prayer and reading my Bible, and that these things will result in me becoming more and more like Jesus. In Jesus' name, I pray, Amen.

NOTES

_____

_____

_____

_____

_____

Obey God's Word

TODAY'S TRUTH: As a follower of Jesus, you express your love to Him by obeying His teachings.

MAIN SCRIPTURE: John 14:15,21

"If you love me, you will keep my commands. … The one who has my commands and keeps them is the one who loves me. And the one who loves me will be loved by my Father. I also will love him and will reveal myself to him" (John 14:15,21).

As a new follower of Christ, you're now in a relationship with Him. Like any relationship, you develop and cultivate your relationship with Christ as you walk daily with Him. Your relationship with Him begins when you recognize that Jesus is Lord (Romans 10:9-10). Jesus is unlike anyone else; because of this, the Bible gives Him the title *Lord*. The word *Lord* means "master" or "boss." The idea that Jesus is Lord means He is in charge, He is in control, and He calls the shots. Your response to His lordship is to obey and keep His commands, and to say yes to Him when He speaks to you through His Word and through prayer. It means that you know His teachings and follow them. When you experience tension between what you desire to do and what Jesus says you should do, you yield to Him.

How would you describe Jesus to someone who doesn't know Him?

_____

_____

One way we express our love for God is to obey His commands that we find in Scripture. We typically think of a mom or dad trying to teach a small child when we see the words "obey" or "obedience." Parents are entrusted with the responsibility of raising their children and caring for them. One aspect of parenting involves teaching children the difference between right and wrong. Another aspect of developing a healthy parent-child relationship and demonstrating love requires setting boundaries and rules for the child's safety.

Our relationship with God works in a similar way. He loves us deeply, so much so that He places boundaries and rules for our benefit. Our love for God makes us want to obey Him, and Scripture says we will be blessed when we do. Our obedience to God is an outward expression of our trust in Him that He knows what is best for us.

The good news is we don't have to wonder what God wants us to do. God's commands are found in the Bible. It's important that as a new believer you begin to read the Bible. In the Word of God, you'll learn what He tells us to do and how we are to live. You will discover that God is pleased when you follow His commands. As your relationship with Jesus grows, you express your love and devotion to Him by keeping His commands.

Jesus talked about our obedience in John 14:15: "If you love me, then you will keep my commands." This sentence has the feel of an if/then statement: *If* we love Him, *then* we will keep His commands. While that is true, the word "if" in this passage can be understood as *since*. "[Since] you love me, you will keep my commands" (John 14:15). This meaning is clear when you read the words of Jesus in John 14:21: "The one who has my commands and keeps them is the one who loves me. And the one who loves me will be loved by my Father. I also will love him and will reveal myself to him."

Why do you think our obedience matters to God?

_____

_____

What part of obeying God's Word seems difficult to you right now?

_____

_____

So, where should you begin? One of the first things Jesus asks you to do as a new Christian is to be baptized. In Matthew 28:19, Jesus commanded His followers to make disciples and to baptize them. The Book of Acts tells the story of the very first Christians who established the church after Jesus' death and resurrection. Those who came to faith in Christ were baptized to demonstrate their commitment to follow Him. It's the same for you. Jesus commands His followers to be baptized as an outward expression of their commitment to follow Him. Being baptized is one of your first steps of obedience to His commands.

PRAYER: Father, thank You for inviting me to be in a relationship with You. Help me to understand Your Word so that I can obey what it says. May my actions and words demonstrate my love for You. When I struggle to follow Your way, remind me of Your constant love that desires the best for me. In Jesus' name, I pray, Amen.

NOTES

_____

_____

_____

_____

_____

Get Connected

TODAY'S TRUTH: You are not meant to live the Christian life alone.

MAIN SCRIPTURE: Hebrews 10:24-25

Rock climbing is a demanding sport in which the participant climbs up a rock ledge using whatever handholds and footholds he can find. The journey is dangerous and laden with potential hazards, leading seasoned rock climbers to suggest one thing: Don't climb alone. A partner, positioned on the ground holding the belay rope wrapped around him, can support the climber's weight if he slips. Having a partner allows the climber to experience climbs he couldn't attempt on his own. In the same way, God's Word teaches us that we were never meant to live out our faith in isolation. The Christian life is meant to be lived alongside other Christians.

When God created us, He made us for relationships. In fact, our lives are filled with them: smartphones connect us to friends and family; social media platforms allow us to communicate with friends from all seasons of our lives; and refrigerators hold pictures of those people whom add meaning to our lives. These relationships are a significant part of life. However, now your most significant relationship is the one you have with Jesus, because only Jesus is able to save you from your sin.

Our relationship with Jesus shapes all of our other relationships, especially our relationships with other Christians. As we learn about what it means to follow Jesus, we cannot overlook this vital truth: God never intended for us to live the Christian life alone. We were made for Christian community, living our day-to-day lives alongside other Christians. Hebrews 10:24-25 reminds us of the importance of the church: "And let us watch out for one another to provoke love and good works, not neglecting to gather together, as some are in the habit of doing, but encouraging each other, and all the more as you see the day approaching."

Who was instrumental in teaching you about Jesus? How did he or she do this?

_____

_____

_____

Following Jesus is a personal decision that leads us to do things like pray, read God's Word, and worship. These things are invaluable because they help us to grow spiritually. However, it is equally important to grow spiritually alongside other Christians. When we get involved in a local church we immediately benefit. With other Christians, we:

- Grow in our understanding of the Bible;
- Pray for each other;
- Encourage others and receive encouragement;
- Serve alongside others to fulfill God-given tasks;
- Learn from others what it looks like to trust and follow God.

What is one prayer request you would like someone to pray for with you? Who can you ask to join you in praying for this need?

_____

_____

_____

How have you connected with other Christians? In what specific ways have they encouraged or challenged you in your faith?

_____

_____

_____

In 1 Corinthians 12:12,27, the apostle Paul describes the church as a body that has many parts. In the same way, the church is made up of many Christians who have different skills and abilities. We are called to build and prioritize healthy relationships with other Christians because we need each other. Simply put, there are some things about following Jesus that we can only learn in the context of our relationships with other Christians. As we read God's Word, pray, worship, and serve with other Christians, God unifies and equips us to follow Him more closely each day.

PRAYER: Father, thank You for designing me for relationships that bring joy and fullness to my life. I'm grateful to be part of Your family. Help me to prioritize getting involved with my church and forging strong relationships with other followers of Jesus who love You too. Show me, through other Christians, what it means to trust You in the ups and downs of life, when challenges come, and when great things happen. Allow me to see when and how I can encourage someone else. In Jesus' name, I pray, Amen.

NOTES

_____

_____

God's Promise of Eternal Life

TODAY'S TRUTH: God wants you to know with confidence
that you have eternal life.

MAIN SCRIPTURE: 1 John 5:11-13

We want to end this week with this promise: those who become followers of Jesus are given
the promise of eternal life. One of the most well-known verses in the Bible is John 3:16: "For God
loved the world in this way: He gave his one and only Son, so that everyone who believes in him
will not perish but have eternal life."

When people hear the words "eternal life" they almost always think of heaven. In this instance
that's exactly what Jesus is referring to. By placing your faith in Jesus, you have the promise
of heaven. Death is not the end of the story for Christians. There is more to life than our earthly
existence. Eternal life means that God is with us now and we will be in heaven with Him forever.

**What do you find most hopeful or encouraging about the truth that
God offers us eternal life?**

_____

_____

_____

_____

God promises eternal life for those who follow Him. He wants us to be confident in His promise.
In 1 John 5:11-13, we're reassured of this: "And this is the testimony: God has given us eternal
life, and this life is in his Son. The one who has the Son has life. The one who does not have the
Son of God does not have life. I have written these things to you who believe in the name of the
Son of God so that you may know that you have eternal life."

John wrote these words so that you would know for certain that you have eternal life when
you believe in Jesus. We want you to know from the outset of the journey of following Jesus
that along the way you will encounter doubts, questions, challenges, and feelings of insecurity
regarding your eternal destiny. God gives assurance that eternity is guaranteed because you
believe in Jesus. It's not about what you do from this point forward. You cannot earn eternal
life. You don't deserve it. It's His gift to those who believe in Jesus. You cannot lose it because
of mistakes you make, missteps you take, or sins you commit. Your sins are forgiven—past,
present, and future.

Nothing can take away God's promise of eternal life to those who believe in Jesus. Nothing can change that fact. Jesus said to His followers: "My sheep hear my voice, I know them, and they follow me. I give them eternal life, and they will never perish. No one will snatch them out of my hand. My Father, who has given them to me, is greater than all. No one is able to snatch them out of the Father's hand" (John 10:27-29).

What do these verses teach us about God's character and power?

_____

_____

_____

_____

The apostle Paul encouraged us to have unwavering faith: "Who can separate us from the love of Christ? Can affliction or distress or persecution or famine or nakedness or danger or sword? ... For I am persuaded that neither death nor life, nor angels nor rulers, nor things present nor things to come, nor powers, nor height nor depth, nor any other created thing will be able to separate us from the love of God that is in Christ Jesus our Lord" (Romans 8:35,38-39).

There may be times when you feel insecure about the decision to follow Christ. In moments of doubt or questioning, you might wonder to yourself, _Can it be true that I will live forever in heaven because I am a follower of Jesus?_ These types of questions, doubts, and fears are not unusual for new believers. We will talk about the reasons for this in future sessions, but these words of Scripture were given so you will know with certainty that eternal life is yours and nothing can take that away. As a Christian, you belong to God and you have the promise of eternal life with Him forever.

PRAYER: Father, thank You for the gift of Your presence both today and forever in heaven. I want to have an unwavering faith in the promises You give me in Your Word. When questions or doubts arise, help me to always seek Your Word for truth. Help me to turn to Your Word each day so it will become the foundation of my life. In Jesus' name, I pray, Amen.

NOTES

_____

_____

_____

_____

Week 1 Journal

Use these pages to journal as you go through the week. If you need guidance, use the following questions to help you.

What truths or promises from God's Word stood out to you this week?

_____

_____

_____

_____

_____

What did you learn about God this week?

_____

_____

_____

_____

_____

How can you obey or apply what you have learned from God's Word this week?

_____

_____

_____

_____

_____

What prayer requests do you have?

_____

_____

_____

_____

_____

_____

_____

_____

_____

_____

_____

_____

_____

_____

_____

_____

_____

_____

_____

_____

_____

WEEKLY TRUTH TO MEMORIZE:

Therefore, if anyone is in Christ, he is a new creation; the old has passed away, and see, the new has come! 2 Corinthians 5:17

MY NEW LIFE

Understanding the Gospel

For I passed on to you as most important what I also received: that Christ died for our sins according to the Scriptures, that he was buried, that he was raised on the third day according to the Scriptures.

1 CORINTHIANS 15:3-4

MAIN IDEA:

Jesus died for our sins so that we can be forgiven and live in relationship with God now and for eternity.

WEEK 2

. . .

MY NEW LIFE

There Is One True God

TODAY'S TRUTH: God created the world and everything in it. He is perfect, holy, and all-powerful.

MAIN SCRIPTURE: Acts 17:24-31

In the next two weeks, we want to take you on a short journey into the Scriptures to be sure you understand some very basic truths about two foundational aspects of the Christian life, which are essential to your development as a new believer. First, we want you to have a clear understanding of the gospel. We have made reference to the gospel in previous weeks, but this will be a deeper dive into this fundamental teaching: Jesus died for our sins so that we can be forgiven and live in relationship with God—now and for eternity.

Second, we want you to have a basic understanding of who God is, which will include focusing on His nature and character. You will discover that there is only one God, the good and loving Creator of all things, who exists as three persons—the Father, the Son, and the Holy Spirit.

In Acts 17, the apostle Paul was in Athens, speaking to a group of people when he made this point about God: "The God who made the world and everything in it—he is Lord of heaven and earth—does not live in shrines made by hands. Neither is he served by human hands, as though he needed anything, since he himself gives everyone life and breath and all things. From one man he has made every nationality to live over the whole earth and has determined their appointed times and the boundaries of where they live" (Acts 17:24-26).

God is the Creator of the world and everything in it. The people of Athens worshiped idols of false gods, but Paul sought to point them to the one true God. Paul stated clearly that God does not need anything from human beings, but we are the ones who are in great need of Him. In fact, God has given us the very breath that we live by. Paul went on in this passage to explain that God, as our Creator, has designed the whole world to point to Him, including every person that has ever lived: "He did this so that they might seek God, and perhaps they might reach out and find him, though he is not far from each one of us" (Acts 17:27).

What does Acts 17:24-27 teach us about God's power and authority over His creation?

_____

_____

_____

In verse 30, Paul made it clear that God commands people to repent of their sin and that He will be the final judge over the whole earth. As our Creator, God has complete authority over our lives. All people have sinned, but we are called to confess, repent, and seek God's forgiveness. We should be motivated by the truth that one day God will judge everyone who has ever lived. Unlike humans, God is perfect in everything He does and He will judge us by His standard, not ours.

Finally, Paul told those in Athens that God has provided final proof of His authority through the resurrection of Jesus from the dead. "God now commands all people everywhere to repent, because he has set a day when he is going to judge the world in righteousness by the man he has appointed. He has provided proof of this to everyone by raising him from the dead" (Acts 17:30-31). God is perfect, holy, and all-powerful. He has sent His Son, Jesus, to earth so we would turn from our sin and turn to Him.

Where do you see evidence of God's power and authority in His creation?

_____

_____

_____

We can take great joy in the fact that we worship the one true and living God. Unlike the false gods of other religions, our God does not need anything from us but has given us everything we could ever need because of His great love for us. As we seek to trust God more and follow Him daily, He will make us more like Him in holiness.

PRAYER: Pray and thank God that He is perfectly holy and right in everything He does. Thank Him that by His power He has created everything and everyone on the earth. Acknowledge that God has authority over everything, including you. Ask Him to help you dedicate your life to worshiping and following Him.

NOTES

_____

_____

_____

_____

_____

All People Sin

TODAY'S TRUTH: All people reject God in their heart, mind, and actions.

MAIN SCRIPTURE: Psalm 14:1-3

Most people, if asked, would say about themselves, "I am a good person." Not only do we believe our own hearts are good, but we oftentimes say the same of others. The Bible, however, presents us with a different perspective that turns our thinking upside down. In Psalm 14:3, David wrote, "There is no one who does good, not even one." Paul, in Romans 3, quoted David's words by stating, "There is no one righteous, not even one. There is no one who understands; there is no one who seeks God. … There is no one who does what is good, not even one" (Romans 3:10-12). Taking it one step further, Jeremiah 17:9 states, "The heart is more deceitful than anything else, and incurable—who can understand it?"

It is difficult for us to fathom these words in Scripture because in comparison to so many other people, we believe deep down that we are good. We live our lives believing that if we do good things—such as give to the needy, go to church, treat people the way we would like to be treated, remain faithful to our spouse, and so on—then deep down we are a good person.

Our sin will always create a distance or separation between God and ourselves. How have you experienced this in your life?

_____

_____

_____

From the very beginning, with Adam and Eve's sin in the garden of Eden (Genesis 3), our hearts have turned away from God instead of seeking after Him. Thus, our hearts are corrupt. It is vital to understand the condition of our hearts. One of the hard truths the Bible puts before us is that every single person who has ever lived is a sinner. Everyone, by choice and in his or her very nature, has done what God says we should not do. Our sin has broken our relationship with God.

Apart from Jesus, our hearts are inherently deceptive. Throughout our lives, these hearts have led us to believe lies about who we are and why we do what we do. Our hearts deceive us into thinking that what is bad for us is good for us or that God does not love us and we are beyond forgiveness. However, when we begin to acknowledge our own sin, we find forgiveness and acceptance from God. If you are reading this now, our hope is that you have experienced God's forgiveness and acceptance!

There is only one way for our hearts to be healed. There is only one way to be in relationship with God after the separation from Him that our sin has caused. There is only one way to be set free from the sin that has so corrupted our hearts. The answer is Jesus, the one you have chosen to place your trust in. In Romans 7, the apostle Paul said, "Oh, what a miserable person I am! Who will free me from this life that is dominated by sin and death? Thank God! The answer is in Jesus Christ our Lord" (Romans 7:24-25a, New Living Translation).

How would you describe the state of your heart prior to placing your trust in Jesus? How has this changed?

_____

_____

_____

_____

We are broken people living in a broken world; we sin. Thankfully, God offers us forgiveness because of what Christ has done on the cross. Forgiveness is a precious gift, and it begins with confession. When the believer humbly admits to God how he has sinned against Him, he is forgiven. The truth is that we are sinners and that God willingly forgives those who admit their sin. When we confess our sins, we are to then repent, or turn from that sin, and turn to Jesus. Repentance is a heartfelt sorrow for sin, a renouncing of that sin, and a sincere commitment to turn from it and walk in obedience to Christ.

PRAYER: Use the words of Psalm 139:23-24 as you pray: "Search me, God, and know my heart; test me and know my concerns. See if there is any offensive way in me; lead me in the everlasting way." In your own words, ask God to show you the areas of your heart that are not honoring Him. Ask Him to lead your heart as you surrender it to Him.

NOTES

_____

_____

_____

_____

_____

Jesus Died in Our Place

TODAY'S TRUTH: Jesus' death paid the penalty for our sin and
made it possible for us to be counted righteous.

MAIN SCRIPTURE: 2 Corinthians 5:21

In the heart of the Great Depression, the mayor of New York City was a man by the name of
Fiorello La Guardia. In January of 1935, La Guardia took over the bench of a night court in the
city and heard the case of a woman charged with stealing bread. The woman shared that she
stole the bread to feed her grandchildren, who were in desperate need. La Guardia told the
woman he could not ignore the law and must either fine her ten dollars or sentence her to ten
days in jail. As he pronounced the penalty, he worked his hand into his pocket and pulled out
the ten dollars to pay the penalty on behalf of the woman. Further, he charged everyone in the
courtroom fifty cents each for living in a town that forced a woman to steal bread so that her
grandchildren could eat. As the story goes, the woman left the courtroom with her penalty paid
and in a better state than she had entered.

In this story of La Guardia, we see a picture of the gospel message. All mankind, like the woman
in the story, is guilty of sin and in need of grace. As we have discussed this week, God has all
authority over our lives, but people have rejected the truth about God and have instead trusted
in their own wisdom and ways. Like La Guardia in the story, God is unable to ignore the penalty
that must be paid for sin. If God were to ignore our sin, He would not be just. In our sinful state,
there is no way that we could be restored to a right relationship with God. It should be clear, our
sinful state before God is much worse than the state of the grandmother in the story who stood
before the judge.

What does 2 Corinthians 5:21 teach us about sin and how God views it?

_____

_____

_____

Yet, God has not left us in our helpless state. John 3:16 tells us, "For God loved the world in this
way: He gave his one and only Son, so that everyone who believes in him will not perish but
have eternal life." God loves us so much that He made a way that we could be restored to a
relationship with Him. To be clear, this is nothing we deserve. God would have been perfectly
right to condemn all people to hell, separated from Him forever. The Bible makes it abundantly
clear that God was motivated by His great love to make a way for salvation. "For God did not
send his Son into the world to condemn the world, but to save the world through him. Anyone
who believes in him is not condemned, but anyone who does not believe is already condemned,
because he has not believed in the name of the one and only Son of God" (John 3:17-18).

In 2 Corinthians 5:21, Paul stated clearly the way that God provided for salvation: "He made the one who did not know sin to be sin for us, so that in him we might become the righteousness of God." God sent Jesus, who was sinless, to pay our penalty by dying on the cross. And what is the result of this according to 2 Corinthians 5:21? We are counted as righteous before God. Truly, this is good news!

Only Jesus is able to pay for our sins because only Jesus was able to live a perfectly, sinless life on the earth. If Jesus had sin of His own, He would not be an acceptable sacrifice for the sin of mankind. Because Jesus had no sin of His own, He was able to pay for our sin. Further, He gave His perfect life in exchange for our sinful one. On the cross, Jesus took our penalty and gave us His righteousness.

How would you summarize 2 Corinthians 5:21 in your own words?
What do you find most encouraging about this verse?

_____

_____

_____

_____

_____

We can trust the truth found in Romans 8:1, which tells us that there is no condemnation for those who are in Christ Jesus. On the cross, Jesus accepted the punishment for our sin. Indeed, once we are saved by faith in Christ, God loves us and is pleased with us completely. God's love for us does not waver because it is not based on what we do but on what Jesus has done. This is the heart of the gospel and the best news the world has ever known.

PRAYER: Thank God for the glorious truth of the gospel and the great exchange of Jesus' righteousness for our sinfulness. Ask God to help you believe that He is perfectly pleased with those in Christ not based on their merit, but on the perfect merit of Jesus.

NOTES

_____

_____

_____

_____

_____

Jesus Is the Only Way

TODAY'S TRUTH: There is only one way to God: salvation through Jesus.

MAIN SCRIPTURE: John 14:6; Acts 4:12

As we consider living the Christian life, it is vitally important that we keep our focus on the one way that God has given to enter His kingdom: Jesus. To be clear, this does not mean that we have to clean ourselves up for Jesus to accept us and offer forgiveness for our sins. Jesus freely accepts all who repent of their sins and come to Him in faith.

Yesterday, we reflected on the truth that Jesus died in our place so that we could be forgiven for our sins and restored to a right relationship with God. We must always keep our focus on this truth—it is the heart of the gospel. If we are not careful, we will naturally seek to earn God's love by our own good deeds and thinking we are accepted by Him based on what we do instead of what He has done.

However, our attempts to earn our salvation by being "good" will never be enough. Jesus is the only one who could pay for our sins because He is the only one who has ever lived a sinless life. Due to our sinfulness, we can never become righteous enough to reach God on our own.

What are some ways that people try to be "good enough" to earn salvation?

_____

_____

_____

_____

In John 10:7-9, Jesus made it clear that He is the gate by which people enter the kingdom of God: "Truly I tell you, I am the gate for the sheep. All who came before me are thieves and robbers, but the sheep didn't listen to them. I am the gate. If anyone enters by me, he will be saved and will come in and go out and find pasture." There are many people who would say that people can find their way to God through many different ways and different religious beliefs. However, this is not what the Bible says.

Jesus proclaimed this again clearly: "I am the way, the truth, and the life. No one comes to the Father except through me" (John 14:6). Jesus is the only way to salvation because He alone was the perfect, sinless sacrifice. Many people find this kind of exclusive claim about Jesus unacceptable, but as faithful followers of Jesus, we must hold firmly to this truth of the Bible.

How would you summarize Jesus' teaching in John 14:6 in your own words?

_____

_____

_____

_____

In Acts 4, Peter and John were facing persecution due to the message they preached about Jesus. It would have been tempting to take the path of least resistance in this moment and to deny the truth about Jesus. Yet, Peter and John remained faithful to the truth of God and stated clearly that there is no way to salvation apart from Jesus. "There is salvation in no one else, for there is no other name under heaven given to people by which we must be saved" (Acts 4:12).

What makes Jesus stand apart from every other religious figure?

_____

_____

_____

No other person or religious leader offers us salvation from our sins. While others may view this claim as harmful, exclusive, or the gospel as needlessly offensive, we should recognize God's grace in this truth. Not only has God extended grace to mankind by sending Jesus to die in our place and for our sins, but He has shown us grace by telling us clearly that there is no other way to Him apart from Jesus. We show love and grace to others by sharing this truth with them.

PRAYER: Thank God that Jesus has died on the cross so that we could be made right with Him. Thank God that He has clearly revealed that Jesus is the only way to Him and has shown us the path to righteousness in Christ. Pray that you will be faithful to tell others the truth about Jesus.

NOTES

_____

_____

_____

_____

We Respond to Christ by Faith

TODAY'S TRUTH: We're saved when we turn from our sin and by faith trust in Christ.

MAIN SCRIPTURE: Romans 10:9-10

Odds are that you are reading this because you have chosen to respond to Christ by faith. You have chosen to turn from your old way of life and have confessed that Jesus is now the Lord of your life. In your time as a Christian, you have come to see more and more what He has done for you and just how much you need Him.

A few days ago, we discussed the false idea that our hearts are generally good. Not only is there the belief that our hearts are good, but if you were to ask a random sampling of people how they get to heaven, most people would say it's by being a good person. As we discussed this week, two widespread misconceptions about heaven are that there are many ways to get there and you get there by doing more good things than bad things. Unfortunately, these misconceptions contradict what God's Word says. We are saved by grace. Grace is God's unmerited favor, which means we don't deserve it and that God gives it to us anyway. It is God's grace that is the true path to eternity in heaven. The truth of the gospel is that none of us will ever be good enough to get to heaven by our own efforts. We desperately need God's saving grace to make heaven our future reality.

How would you describe God's grace? What has it meant to you?

_____

_____

In Romans 10:9, Paul teaches us that we must confess with our mouth that Jesus is Lord. "If you confess with your mouth, 'Jesus is Lord,' and believe in your heart that God raised him from the dead, you will be saved." This means as a believer we are to declare that Jesus is the Lord of everything, even of those who do not believe. Our confession is that Jesus Christ is Lord over the universe, and that up until our repentance, we had ignored His rightful lordship over our lives. Jesus is Lord, and best of all, He is a good, faithful, and a merciful King who will forgive everyone who confesses and repents of their sins.

Paul also teaches us that we must believe that God raised Jesus from the dead. A savior who is still dead does us no good. Jesus, however, is risen from the dead and is now at the right hand of God the Father. Because Jesus is alive, we have the assurance that one day God will also raise us from the dead. Paul teaches that this good news is available for all people (Romans 10:13).

Everyone who calls upon the name of the Lord will be saved. But to be saved we have to exhibit faith in Jesus. The gospel requires a response.

Once we know that God is holy, that we are not, and that Jesus is the answer, we are to respond. This step in the gospel is the necessity of faith. God has done all of the work and is now asking us to respond to Him in trust. When we take that step of trust toward Jesus, we do so by faith. Saving faith involves repentance, which is turning *from* sin and *to* Christ. Repentance carries with it the idea of doing a 180-degree turn. Picture a road sign with the U-turn arrow for a moment. This is a simple yet clear visual of repentance. It is heading in one direction (a life of sin, separated from God) and choosing to turn away from that life and to a new life in Jesus. This is not a flippant choice, as you know. This response is one that will change (and hopefully already has) your life completely!

When did you respond to the gospel? What do you remember about that day?

_____

_____

How has your life changed since you responded to Jesus in faith?

_____

_____

Now, to be absolutely clear, this response of faith is not a one-time thing. Far too many people have "asked Jesus into their heart," thinking they have punched their ticket to heaven, and then gone right back to living their lives without Him. Responding to God in faith is a daily, ongoing trust in the risen Jesus. It's a daily expression of faith and response to the gospel. Jesus does not just want a one-time commitment, but a lifetime of ongoing trust. What an incredible God we serve that desires continued relationship with us as we trust Him with all that we have!

PRAYER: Praise God for the forgiveness of our sin that He offers through Jesus. Confess to God what you believe about Jesus and what He's taught you about grace. Do not worry about using "correct" words or phrases. God knows your heart and will understand what you are trying to communicate.

NOTES

_____

_____

_____

Week 2 Journal

Use these pages to journal as you go through the week. If you need guidance, use the following questions to help you.

What truths or promises from God's Word stood out to you this week?

_____

_____

_____

_____

_____

What did you learn about God this week?

_____

_____

_____

_____

_____

How can you obey or apply what you have learned from God's Word this week?

_____

_____

_____

_____

_____

What prayer requests do you have?

_____

_____

_____

_____

_____

_____

_____

_____

_____

_____

_____

_____

_____

_____

_____

_____

_____

_____

_____

_____

WEEKLY TRUTH TO MEMORIZE:

For I passed on to you as most important what I also received: that Christ died for our sins according to the Scriptures, that he was buried, that he was raised on the third day according to the Scriptures. 1 Corinthians 15:3-4

Knowing God

The LORD is compassionate and gracious, slow to anger and abounding in faithful love. He will not always accuse us or be angry forever. He has not dealt with us as our sins deserve or repaid us according to our iniquities. For as high as the heavens are above the earth, so great is his faithful love toward those who fear him.

PSALM 103:8-11

MAIN IDEA:

There is only one God, the good and loving Creator of all things, who exists as three persons—the Father, the Son, and the Holy Spirit.

WEEK 3

MY NEW LIFE

God's Character

TODAY'S TRUTH: God is eternal, good, and loving.

MAIN SCRIPTURE: Exodus 34:5-7

"What's in a name? That which we call a rose by any other name would smell as sweet."

These are the words of Juliet to Romeo in the well-known William Shakespeare play, *Romeo and Juliet*. In this Western classic, these two young people—a pair of star-crossed lovers—belong to rival medieval-Italian families, the Capulets and Montagues. Compelled by love and desperation, the two go to drastic lengths to marry that result in outright tragedy. While people's names are commonly invested with meaning, they do not necessarily match the life and character of the persons to whom they are given. Thankfully, this is not the case with God. The Bible gives us a different and non-tragic answer to Juliet's question, "What's in a name?"

In Exodus 34:5-7, the name that God revealed to the prophet Moses aligns precisely with who God is: He is eternal, good, and loving. "The Lord is a compassionate and gracious God, slow to anger and abounding in faithful love and truth, maintaining faithful love to a thousand generations, forgiving iniquity, rebellion, and sin. But he will not leave the guilty unpunished" (Exodus 34:6b-7a).

In the sequence of events that led to revealing His name, Moses implored God to see His glory—a way of requesting a tangible display of who God is (Exodus 33:18). In other words, Moses was asking the age-old question, "What is God like?" In this case, however, he happened to be asking the question directly to God.

In this passage, along with several thousand others, God's personal name, *Yahweh*, is translated "Lord" in all capital letters, a typical occurrence in most English Bibles. This translation of "Yahweh" mimics an ancient Jewish practice done to revere God's name. In Hebrew (one of the languages in which the Bible was originally written), the name Yahweh is drawn from another way that God referred to Himself when Moses first met Him: "I AM WHO I AM" (3:14). God then reiterated His name again in verse 15: "The Lord" (or "Yahweh"). His very name tells us of His self-existence: "I AM WHO I AM."

First, God's name (Yahweh) reveals His eternal nature. He transcends time and space, having no beginning and no end. He is infinite; He is eternal. Yahweh's name leads us to consider Him as the independent Creator who stands in need of nothing and also as the covenant Lord on whom we depend for everything.

What do you find encouraging about the fact that God is eternal?

_____

_____

Second, God reveals His goodness in terms of His grace and love. Exodus 34:6-7 reveals the multifaceted ways in which God shows Himself as loving and gracious to us. Indeed, He is "compassionate and gracious" (Exodus 34:6). Grace is favor that we do not deserve, and as sinners, we depend on God's constant compassion, mercy, and patience, none of which we deserve. Further, God reserves this display of love not merely for a few but for the many, even to "a thousand generations" (Exodus 34:7), asserting His willingness to pardon the widest range of offenses against Him: "forgiving iniquity, rebellion, and sin" (Exodus 34:7).

Third, God reveals His goodness in terms of His just judgments. God is good, and He will punish evil. Like good judges in the human realm who pass deserved sentences on convicted criminals, God is a good Judge who "will not leave the guilty unpunished" (Exodus 34:7), a truth that points us to the cross itself where Jesus stood in the place of the guilty so that sinners could be forgiven. While God does not punish individuals for the specific sins of their parents (Ezekiel 18:20), there are nonetheless consequences for sin whose effects go beyond the individual sinner. God's goodness is reflected in His judgment of sin and especially in Jesus' death on the cross.

Which of the descriptions of God given in Exodus 34:5-7 are more meaningful for you today? Why?

_____

_____

What's in a name? When it comes to God's name, quite a bit. In Exodus 34, God describes His name and character as eternal, good, and loving. When it comes to Yahweh, no other "rose" smells as sweet; no other is worthy of this name.

PRAYER: Praise God for being good, eternal, and loving. Thank God for the gracious compassion He shows His people and for the way you've experienced this in your relationship with Him.

NOTES

_____

_____

Creator

TODAY'S TRUTH: The eternal triune God is the good and loving Creator of all things.

MAIN SCRIPTURE: Genesis 1:1

"In the beginning ..." (Genesis 1:1).

These three words form the foundation of our understanding of the Creator and creation. God is the One who formed everything in the universe, what Genesis 1:1 calls "the heavens and the earth."

As we learned yesterday, the God who spoke to Moses is eternal in nature, not having a beginning or end. This same God who revealed His name as Yahweh, "I AM WHO I AM," is the God who created the world, all things visible and invisible. He is not one among many gods but the one true God who brought everything else into existence; He is the "Lord God" who delivered the Israelites out of slavery in Egypt (Exodus 20:2-3). Accordingly, Genesis 1:1 introduces us to the eternal, good, and loving Creator: "In the beginning God created the heavens and the earth" (Genesis 1:1).

We are first introduced in Genesis 1:1 to God as the eternal Creator. To create something, someone must "preexist" that something. For example, builders preexist houses. Unlike builders—who produce things *out of* and *from* other things—God created *out of nothing* and *from nothing*. This demonstrates that God is the Creator and we are but His creation; we were created, He was not. He can tell us about the beginning because He was there—before there was a there and before there was a before: "Before the mountains were born, before you gave birth to the earth and the world, from eternity to eternity, you are God" (Psalm 90:2). Yahweh, the God of Israel, is the God who was, is, and will forever be.

What does it mean for us that God created all things?

_____

_____

_____

Additionally, we are introduced in Genesis 1:1 to God as the good Creator. The first chapter of Genesis tells us six times that God "saw" that specific aspects of His creation were good (Genesis 1:4,10,12,18,21,25). After He created humanity, He pronounced all of creation "very good" (Genesis 1:31). The always-good Creator is by nature always good to His creation. And because He is eternal, time and space are no obstacles for Him to overcome in expressing His goodness to us. Even His love transcends time and space itself: "For as high as the heavens are above the earth, so great is his faithful love toward those who fear him" (Psalm 103:11). God is good, His creation is good, and He treats His good creation according to His goodness: "Every good and perfect gift is from above, coming down from the Father of lights, who does not change like shifting shadows" (James 1:17).

We are, moreover, introduced in Genesis 1:1 to God as the loving Creator. God is not only good to us, but He loves us as well. Genesis 1 paints a picture for the reader of God preparing a fully furnished and well-functioning home for His creation: the sky for the birds, the water for the fish, and the land for humans and animals. Elsewhere in Scripture, we see the extent of God's love for human beings by the way that He cares for all of them, even His enemies: "For he causes his sun to rise on the evil and the good, and sends rain on the righteous and the unrighteous" (Matthew 5:45). God loves us to the furthest extent, even to the point that He willingly allowed His Son to experience death itself for our sake (1 John 4:9-10).

How have you seen evidence of God's love for His people this week?

_____

_____

_____

Lastly, we are introduced in Genesis 1:1 to God as the triune Creator. This eternal, good, and loving God we read about here in Genesis 1 is the same God we read about in the New Testament—one God who exists eternally as the Father, the Son, and the Holy Spirit. "Triune" ("three in one") is a term Christians have used for nearly two millennia to talk about God as the Trinity. God is one being who exists as three persons, a truth that is hinted at here in the opening two chapters of Genesis. We will look more at the Trinity in the following three days, focusing on the Father, the Son, and the Holy Spirit each day.

PRAYER: Thank God for being the Creator of all things, from the depths of the seas to the heavens above. Pay attention to what you see in creation today and what it reveals to you about our Creator. Then, praise Him for making all things.

NOTES

_____

_____

_____

_____

_____

. . .

The Father

TODAY'S TRUTH: God is a good and loving heavenly Father toward His children.

MAIN SCRIPTURE: Matthew 7:7-12

We discover what God is like through what He says and what He does, particularly from His self-revealed name and attributes. In light of Exodus 34 and Genesis 1, we have learned so far that God is the eternal, good, loving, and triune Creator. God's actions and His words show us what He is like. For instance, we have seen that God is good and that we come to know His goodness by His good works: "You are good, and you do what is good" (Psalm 119:68). As an artist's personality shows up in his artwork, so likewise God's goodness shows up in His own works of art, such as His mighty works of creation and salvation. A similar relationship holds true for how we come to know God as Father.

We know God as Father because of His fatherly words and fatherly actions. Though God's fatherhood is not emphasized in the Old Testament as frequently as it is in the New Testament, the Old Testament does in fact teach this concept:

- God referred to Israel as His firstborn son (Exodus 4:22-23);

- God stated that He would call the future descendant of David's line "my son" (2 Samuel 7:12-15); and

- God both identified Himself as Father to Israel and treated them as such: "Keep in mind that the LORD your God has been disciplining you just as a man disciplines his son" (Deuteronomy 8:5).

What are some traits of a good father?

_____

_____

_____

The New Testament then builds on the Old Testament's idea of God as Father, testifying to it widely and emphasizing it with more intensity, beginning with Jesus (John 20:17) and extending to those who become God's children through faith in Jesus (John 1:12-13; Galatians 3:26). In today's Scripture, Jesus spoke of God's goodness and fatherhood being reflected in the way He takes cares of His children: "If you then, who are evil, know how to give good gifts to your children, how much more will your Father in heaven give good things to those who ask him" (Matthew 7:11). Jesus affirms that God is Father to His people by caring for them as His own children. He is a good Father who knows precisely what His children need (Matthew 7:9-10).

How have you seen traits of a good Father displayed in God's Word or His actions?

_____

_____

_____

We also know God as Father because of His Son, Jesus. As strange as it might sound, God did not need us or anything else in creation in order to exist as a Father. God did not become a father but rather revealed Himself to be *the* Father. He has forever existed as the Father. He is the eternal Father of the eternal Son.

This is part of what the apostle John had in mind when he wrote, "In the beginning was the Word, and the Word was with God" (John 1:1-2). The Father and the Son (or Word) have a unique, intimate, and eternal relationship, just as Jesus indicated: "All things have been entrusted to me by my Father. No one knows the Son except the Father, and no one knows the Father except the Son and anyone to whom the Son desires to reveal him" (Matthew 11:27).

Another one of the clearest teachings of God the Father's love for His Son—and even of the Trinity itself, God's existence as Father, Son, and Holy Spirit—is found in Jesus' baptism. "When Jesus was baptized, he went up immediately from the water. The heavens suddenly opened for him, and he saw the Spirit of God descending like a dove and coming down on him. And a voice from heaven said: 'This is my beloved Son, with whom I am well-pleased'" (Matthew 3:16-17).

The same God we read about who spoke to Moses is the same God who spoke the words: "This is my beloved Son" (Matthew 3:17). We will learn more about what it means to believe that God is a Trinity in our next two days. Specifically, tomorrow, we will consider how Jesus, the Son, is uniquely capable of showing us who God is.

PRAYER: Thank God for being a good and loving Father. Praise Him for sending His Son to give us a clearer understanding of who He is and what He is like.

NOTES

_____

_____

_____

_____

• • •

The Son

TODAY'S TRUTH: Jesus is the eternal Son of God who reveals to us
what the Father is like.

MAIN SCRIPTURE: John 1:1-5,14,18

"He's a chip off the old block."

"The apple doesn't fall far from the tree."

"He's the spitting image of his father."

Each of these sayings communicates this truth: sons can be profoundly and eerily like their
fathers. When it comes to Jesus, this proves to be the case. Jesus, the Son of God, was and is
"the radiance of God's glory and the exact expression of his nature" (Hebrews 1:3). Before there
ever was a universe, this Son was the "spitting image" of His Father: "He is the image of the
invisible God" (Colossians 1:15).

As we learned yesterday, we come to know God as Father because of Jesus. At Jesus'
baptism, after the Holy Spirit descended on Him like a dove, the Father declared that Jesus
was His uniquely cherished Son: "This is my beloved Son, with whom I am well-pleased"
(Matthew 3:17). As the church of the early centuries recognized, this passage is foundational
for understanding the Trinity. The Father, the Son, and the Holy Spirit have co-existed in
relationships from before the beginning and without ending. There aren't three gods who
combine to make one bigger God, nor does God take turns playing the roles of Father, Son,
and Holy Spirit. Rather, mysteriously and majestically God exists as one being and also as
three persons eternally and simultaneously.

What do you find most compelling about the Trinity?

_____

_____

_____

The apostle John discusses the beautiful reality of the Trinity in the first chapter of his Gospel:
"In the beginning was the Word, and the Word was with God, and the Word was God" (John
1:1). John then goes on to affirm that like God, the Word is responsible for bringing the universe
into existence: "All things were created through him, and apart from him not one thing was
created that has been created" (John 1:3). Further, the Word sustains creation, giving life to His
creatures and making God's character known to even those who refuse to acknowledge Him:
"In him was life, and that life was the light of men. That light shines in the darkness, and yet the
darkness did not overcome it" (John 1:4-5).

The passage later calls attention to how Jesus reveals God's character: "The Word became flesh and dwelt among us. We observed his glory, the glory as the one and only Son from the Father, full of grace and truth" (John 1:14). The term *flesh* was John's way of referring to human nature. Here, the apostle affirmed that Jesus reveals God to us in a way that nothing else does because of not only His acquired humanity but also because of His special relationship with the Father: "No one has ever seen God. The one and only Son, who is himself God and is at the Father's side—he has revealed him" (John 1:18). As the Son of the Father, Jesus is particularly qualified for showing us who God is. As Jesus said, "The one who has seen me has seen the Father" (John 14:9). Jesus reveals God's character to us because He is eternal, loving, and good in the same way that God is.

How would you summarize the truths found in John 1:14 in your own words?

_____

_____

_____

Jesus, the Son, is eternal, as God is. He identifies Himself as the God of Abraham, the "I AM" who appeared long ago to Moses in the burning bush (John 8:58). Jesus elsewhere prayed that He and the Father share the same eternal, divine glory: "Father, glorify me in your presence with that glory I had with you before the world existed" (John 17:5).

Jesus is loving, as God is. We know the love of God the Father by the love we experience through the Son, again something Jesus prayed about: "I made your name known to them and will continue to make it known, so that the love you have loved me with may be in them and I may be in them" (John 17:26).

Jesus is good, as God is. In His encounter with the rich young ruler, Jesus explained that He is good like God alone is good: "'Why do you call me good?' Jesus asked him. 'No one is good except God alone'" (Luke 18:19). In this conversation, Jesus was not denying His goodness but instead implying His goodness stemmed from His identity. As God's good works reveal and display His goodness, so too do Jesus' works display God's goodness because He is the good God in human form.

PRAYER: Spend time thanking God for sending Jesus to earth so that we might understand God the Father better and grasp the depth of His love and goodness. Praise Jesus for revealing God's character to us.

NOTES

_____

_____

The Holy Spirit

TODAY'S TRUTH: The Father and the Son sent the Holy Spirit to live inside Christians in order to help us live the Christian life.

MAIN SCRIPTURE: John 14:16-17,26

Over the past several days, we have learned through Scripture that God is the eternal, good, and loving Creator. God is one being who has forever existed in three persons: the Father, the Son, and the Holy Spirit. As we come to know God personally as Father and Son because of Jesus, we also come to know that the Holy Spirit is God because of Jesus. The New Testament identifies the Spirit as God (Acts 5:3-4), calling Him by the title "Lord" (2 Corinthians 3:17-18). Indeed, the apostle Paul states that the Spirit is omniscient like God; He knows all things. The Holy Spirit knows God's thoughts as only God does (1 Corinthians 2:10-11). The Spirit is distinct from the Father and the Son and yet also is fully God like the other two persons are.

As we saw with Jesus' baptism, we see the three persons interacting at once with the Father speaking, the Son coming up from the water, and the Spirit descending like a dove (Matthew 3:16-17). Jesus promised that He and His Father would send the Holy Spirit to dwell inside His followers: "And I will ask the Father, and he will give you another Counselor to be with you forever. He is the Spirit of truth. The world is unable to receive him because it doesn't see him or know him. But you do know him, because he remains with you and will be in you. … But the Counselor, the Holy Spirit, whom the Father will send in my name, will teach you all things and remind you of everything I have told you" (John 14:16-17,26).

What do you find encouraging in these verses?

_____

_____

_____

_____

_____

The Spirit, who is God, came to live with and in Jesus' followers—and not the unbelieving world—so we could know God through Him. The Spirit came to teach us about Jesus and to testify about Him. Without the Spirit, we cannot know who God is. The Spirit unites us with the triune God by His coming to live inside of us from the moment of salvation onward (Ephesians 1:13), enabling us to know God (1 Corinthians 2:12), and empowering us to live on mission with Him (Acts 1:8). It is because of Jesus that we came to receive the Spirit as God's adopted children (Galatians 4:4-7).

Jesus prepared His disciples for the Holy Spirit prior to His death, resurrection, and ascension to heaven. It would be the Holy Spirit who would empower them for their mission: "Jesus said to them again, 'Peace be with you. As the Father has sent me, I also send you.' After saying this, he breathed on them and said, 'Receive the Holy Spirit'" (John 20:21-22).

Elsewhere, Jesus made a similar statement: "You will receive power when the Holy Spirit has come on you, and you will be my witnesses in Jerusalem, in all Judea and Samaria, and to the end of the earth" (Acts 1:8).

The Holy Spirit indwells Christians, empowering them to serve and follow God each day. In what current situation do you need to depend on the Holy Spirit?

_____

_____

_____

_____

The Spirit helps us to know God personally and relationally, but that is not where His work in us ends. He helps us to know God and His Word so that we might in turn make God and His Word known to people throughout the world. With our sharing of the gospel with others, we announce the good news that Jesus has done everything necessary to welcome sinners into His kingdom through repentance and faith. By the Spirit, we know God and we make Him known to others.

PRAYER: Thank God for the Holy Spirit and His continued guidance in our lives. Praise Him for giving us godly wisdom, a sense of God's presence with us, and the strength needed to serve God each day.

NOTES

_____

_____

_____

_____

_____

_____

_____

_____

Week 3 Journal

Use these pages to journal as you go through the week. If you need guidance, use the following questions to help you.

What truths or promises from God's Word stood out to you this week?

_____

_____

_____

_____

_____

What did you learn about God this week?

_____

_____

_____

_____

_____

How can you obey or apply what you have learned from God's Word this week?

_____

_____

_____

_____

_____

What prayer requests do you have?

_____

_____

_____

_____

_____

_____
_____
_____
_____
_____
_____
_____
_____
_____
_____
_____
_____

WEEKLY TRUTH TO MEMORIZE:

The Lord is compassionate and gracious, slow to anger and abounding in faithful love. He will not always accuse us or be angry forever. He has not dealt with us as our sins deserve or repaid us according to our iniquities. For as high as the heavens are above the earth, so great is his faithful love toward those who fear him. **Psalm 103:8-11**

Following Jesus

I have been crucified with Christ, and I no longer live, but Christ lives in me. The life I now live in the body, I live by faith in the Son of God, who loved me and gave himself for me.

GALATIANS 2:20

MAIN IDEA:

Christians are called to die to their former way of life and to live by faith in Christ.

WEEK *4*

. . .

MY NEW LIFE

Follow Jesus Daily

TODAY'S TRUTH: At its core, the Christian life is choosing to follow Jesus each day.

MAIN SCRIPTURE: Luke 9:23-26

In the Gospels, we see examples of Jesus boldly walking into the lives of individuals and saying to them, "Follow Me." We see this in two sets of brothers who were fishermen, Peter and Andrew and James and John (Matthew 4:17-22; Mark 1:16-20). Jesus' call required them to walk away from their way of life to follow Him. The same thing happened when Jesus encountered Matthew (called Levi in the Gospels of Mark and Luke) a tax collector, and invited Matthew to follow Him (Matthew 9:9; Mark 2:14; Luke 5:27-28). Matthew's response was to leave his livelihood to join Jesus on His mission. On the other hand, there were those who Jesus invited to follow Him who chose not to do so (Luke 18:18-23).

In Luke 9:23, we find these words of Jesus: "If anyone wants to follow after me, let him deny himself, take up his cross daily, and follow me."

Following Jesus requires action. Because of this, the Christian life is often described as a journey. The first followers of Jesus actually followed Him by walking with Him. Following Jesus is an active, dynamic process. When we follow Jesus, we follow His example and live like He lived. We are disciples who are in training to become more and more like Him.

Who do you know that follows Jesus faithfully? What have you observed from him or her about what it means to be a Christian?

_____

_____

_____

_____

It's important to note that following Jesus is not always easy. He asks us to do some things that are counterintuitive, that go against what is natural for us to do. Our normal tendency is to be selfish, to look out for number one, and to be self-promoting. But Jesus said, "deny yourself" (Luke 9:23). Jesus' words clarify His expectations of those who follow Him, and they are high. Following Jesus means we can't just focus on ourselves, and what we want. This can be difficult because we have trouble denying ourselves those things we desire. For example, we diet for the purpose of losing weight. But it's hard to deny ourselves desserts that we crave. It requires a commitment to abstain from foods we long for and to consume less than we might normally eat.

Jesus made clear that a key component of following Him demands that we "take up our cross daily" (Luke 9:23). We have to understand that He wasn't talking about a piece of jewelry we wear around our neck. To carry one's cross means that we voluntarily give up our lives and die to ourselves for the purpose of identifying with Jesus and living for Him. The cost of following Jesus means that we die to our own will and desires for the purpose of living in accordance with Jesus' commands. We are to do this every day until it eventually becomes a way of life for us.

Jesus continued His teaching, focusing on what we gain by following Him. "For whoever wants to save his life will lose it, but whoever loses his life because of me will save it. For what does it benefit someone if he gains the whole world, and yet loses or forfeits himself? For whoever is ashamed of me and my words, the Son of Man will be ashamed of him when he comes in his glory and that of the Father and the holy angels" (Luke 9:24-26). Here's the good news: when we lose our lives for Jesus sake, then our lives are saved. The result of trying to save our own lives by living for ourselves is that we lose our lives. It's the opposite of how we have lived in the past so it will seem foreign to us, but it is exactly how He intends for us to live.

What part of following Jesus seems challenging to you right now? What part seems easy?

_____

_____

_____

_____

PRAYER: Ask God to help you as you seek to follow Him each and every day. Acknowledge and share with Him the difficulties of denying yourself. Ask Him to change your heart as you desire to live for Him.

NOTES

_____

_____

_____

_____

_____

Remain Connected

TODAY'S TRUTH: We grow spiritually when we remain connected to Jesus.

MAIN SCRIPTURE: John 15:1-8

Several years ago, I traveled to another state for a fall festival at an apple orchard. On the back of the property I noticed a pile of limbs. I found the owner and asked if I could have a limb to take home with me. He allowed me to pick one from the pile and explained that the branch was from an Arkansas Black Apple tree. I jokingly told him I was going to take it home and harvest my own apples from that branch next year.

We know that apples will not grow from that branch again. When the branch was separated from the tree, it died. No new fruit can be produced from that limb.

Jesus taught this principle in John 15:1-8. His imagery was a grapevine, not an apple tree, but the same principle holds true. The purpose of a grapevine is to produce fruit, namely grapes. A gardener works to prune the grapevine so it produces the most fruit possible. The only way a branch of a grapevine can produce fruit is if it stays connected to the grapevine. The grapevine is the source of life for the branch and is essential for the production of fruit.

Jesus said this same principle is true in the life of His followers. "I am the vine; you are the branches. The one who remains in me and I in him produces much fruit, because you can do nothing without me" (John 15:5). We must stay connected to Him if we are going to be productive, healthy Christians. If we are going to produce the fruit of the Spirit (Galatians 5:22-23) we have to stay connected to Him. If we are going to reproduce and see others become followers of Jesus, this will only happen as we stay connected to Him. Jesus is the true source of life, health, vitality, and fruitfulness.

What are some steps we can take to intentionally grow our relationship with Jesus each day?

_____

_____

_____

Jesus invites us to experience life connected to Him always—all of the time, every day. He allows us to enter into a dynamic relationship with Him, where He is with us to help us live the Christian life. The word "remain" communicates the idea of a relationship that continues day after day, regardless of circumstances. In John 14:23, Jesus makes the statement that "If anyone loves me, he will keep my word. My Father will love him, and we will come to him and make our home with him." When we are actively obeying Jesus' teachings, we are connected to Him in such a way that He sets up residence in our lives. He desires an ongoing, daily relationship with us.

This relationship—being continually connected to Jesus—enables us to be healthy and fruitful. "My Father is glorified by this: that you produce much fruit and prove to be my disciples" (John 15:8). On occasion, God will work to cut off or prune things out of our lives so we can be more productive. His goal is to make you more and more into the person He called you to be. By staying connected to Him, God is able to "produce fruit" in us and through us.

The importance of remaining connected to Jesus daily cannot be overstated. Jesus teaches that apart from Him, we can do nothing: "If anyone does not remain in me, he is thrown aside like a branch and he withers. They gather them, throw them into the fire, and they are burned" (John 15:6). No fruit will be produced if we are cut off from Him. A vital, life-giving connection with Jesus is required for healthy, fruitful Christian living. The only good use for wood separated from the tree for fire.

What are the benefits of remaining connected to Jesus every day?

_____

_____

_____

_____

_____

One of the great promises of Jesus to us is: "I am with you always, to the end of the age" (Matthew 28:20). We are never alone; He is always with us. Remaining in Jesus means more than simply recognizing His presence with us. To remain in Christ means that we are connected to Him as our source of life; His love and power flow through us so He can make us healthy, producing the fruit He intends for us to yield.

PRAYER: Thank God for His promise to be with us each day. Commit to set aside time daily for prayer and reading God's Word as a way to prioritize your relationship with Him.

NOTES

_____

_____

_____

_____

_____

Spiritual Disciplines

TODAY'S TRUTH: We commit to daily growth and training in godliness.

MAIN SCRIPTURE: 1 Timothy 4:7-10

Many years ago, a traveling circus arrived in a small town. A circus tent was erected. There was a sense of excitement as the people of the town witnessed elephants, lions, and tigers for the first time ever. Acrobats and other circus personnel marched into the circus tent. It was show time! At one point during the show a trainer entered the ring and started running the tigers through their act. Suddenly the lights went out in the tent. Inside the ring, the trainer continued to lead the tigers through their routine, as if nothing had happened. It became silent in the tent as people listened to the trainer shout out commands and crack his whip. After a few minutes the generators started, the lights came on, and the crowd cheered as the trainer completed his act and the tigers returned to their cages.

After the show, the trainer was asked, "How were you able to remain calm in such a time of fear and suspense?" The tiger trainer replied, "I knew the tigers could see me, but they didn't know I couldn't see them. I knew that my only hope was to continue to take them through the routine they were trained to do just like I normally would do."

The mantra for the disciplined person is "practice, practice, practice." The daily discipline of training in godliness is critical to our success in living the Christian life. The apostle Paul encouraged his young friend, Timothy, with these words: "But have nothing to do with pointless and silly myths. Rather, train yourself in godliness. For the training of the body has limited benefit, but godliness is beneficial in every way, since it holds promise for the present life and also for the life to come" (1 Timothy 4:7-8). We grow in our understanding of God's Word when we spend time studying it. We develop deep faith in God when we take our needs to Him and recognize His answers to our prayers. We labor and strive through disciplined practice for the purpose of godliness. This passage teaches us that physical discipline is of little profit compared to spiritual discipline. The present world is temporal, but the life to come will last forever.

Does growing in godliness sound easy or hard to you? Why?

_____

_____

_____

What are spiritual disciplines? Spiritual disciplines are habits practiced daily that enable Christians to grow spiritually. Many spiritual disciplines are things we do individually, like prayer. Other spiritual disciplines involve other Christians, like being a part of a local church and worshiping together as a group of Christians. Two habits that are incorporated into this book are the habits of Bible reading and prayer. Every day you're invited to read a passage from the Bible that aligns with the main point of the daily reading. At the end of each session, you are encouraged to pray about what you have learned.

The Bible doesn't contain a set list of spiritual disciplines, but it does show us habits and practices that will enable us to grow in godliness:

- **Bible Study:** Spending time studying God's Word and gaining a deeper understanding of what it says.
- **Prayer:** Talking to God in a way that includes praise, thanksgiving, confession, and our needs.
- **Worship:** Honoring God with our praise and worship, both individually and with other Christians.
- **Celebration:** Recognizing when God does something in our lives and giving Him the glory for it.
- **Service:** Serving God by serving other people whom He loves. When we serve their physical, emotional, or spiritual needs, we're honoring God.
- **Fellowship:** Building strong relationships with other Christians.
- **Confession:** Sharing areas of weakness that tempt us to sin, as well as times we have chosen to sin against God. God says He will always extend forgiveness to those who confess: "If we confess our sins, he is faithful and righteous to forgive us our sins and to cleanse us from all unrighteousness" (1 John 1:9).
- **Submission:** Choosing God's desires over ours.[1]

What are some habits you would like to put into practice to grow in godliness?

_____

_____

_____

Godliness is a reverence for God that directs the way a person lives their life. Godliness is seen when our lives exhibit attributes and characteristics consistent with God's nature. That's why it is vital for us to know who God is and what is pleasing to Him. When we choose to daily seek God by practicing spiritual disciplines, He shapes and molds us and deepens our dependence on Him.

PRAYER: Ask God to help you develop daily habits that will help you grow spiritually. Seek Him for strength and consistency as you learn more of how to grow in godliness.

Temptation

TODAY'S TRUTH: Although our hearts are prone to wander toward sin,
God is faithful to give us a way out of temptation.

MAIN SCRIPTURE: 1 Corinthians 10:13

Temptation is a reality for every person. You faced temptation before your new life in Christ, and you will continue to be tempted to sin as a follower of Jesus. Our Scripture passage today confirms this reality: "No temptation has come upon you except what is common to humanity" (1 Corinthians 10:13a). We all have this in common: we each face temptation.

We find the reality of temptation early in the Bible. In Genesis 3, Adam and Eve are in the garden of Eden at the very beginning of creation when they experienced temptation. The bad news is they succumbed to the serpent's enticement and disobeyed God. As descendants of Adam and Eve, we follow the same course of action—we experience temptation, we give in to it, and the consequences of sin continue to this day.

It can be helpful to read what else the Bible teaches us about temptation and sin. We know that the devil is the source of temptation; he wants to see us fail. We must be on guard regarding temptation: "Be sober-minded, be alert. Your adversary the devil is prowling around like a roaring lion, looking for anyone he can devour" (1 Peter 5:8). God is not the source of temptations we face. James 1:13-15 says, "No one undergoing a trial should say, 'I am being tempted by God' since God is not tempted by evil, and he himself doesn't tempt anyone. But each person is tempted when he is drawn away and enticed by his own evil desire. Then after desire has conceived, it gives birth to sin, and when sin is fully grown, it gives birth to death." The writer of Hebrews tells us that Jesus faced all of the same temptations we face yet he did not yield to any of them. Hebrews 4:15 says, "For we do not have a high priest who is unable to sympathize with our weaknesses, but one who has been tempted in every way as we are, yet without sin."

What do these verses teach us about temptation and sin?

_____

_____

_____

The bad news is that we are all sinners and will continue to be tempted to sin. The good news is that Jesus died on the cross for our sins (1 Corinthians 15:3-4). As a new believer, your sins have been forgiven. Even though you are forgiven, you will continue to struggle with temptation. But there is more good news. According to Hebrews 4:15, Jesus understands what it's like to be tempted to sin. He can identify with the struggles we face regarding temptation to sin.

God has sent the Holy Spirit to help you live the life He wants you to live, which includes victory over temptation.

Today's Scripture offers *more* good news. "But God is faithful; he will not allow you to be tempted beyond what you are able, but with the temptation he will also provide a way out so that you may be able to bear it" (1 Corinthians 10:13b). God will provide a way of escape from the temptation to sin. We don't have to give in to the urge or attraction to sin. When we are tempted, we don't have to cave in to the pressure to sin. God will provide a way out and we can overcome the temptations we face.

Why should 1 Corinthians 10:13 give you confidence when you struggle with temptations?

_____

_____

_____

You may have heard someone say, "God will never allow you to experience more than you can handle." The thought is that if some hurtful or tragic thing has happened to you, you can handle it, because God won't allow anything to happen to you that you can't handle. It's a nice thought. It's an attempt to help those who are struggling with overwhelming circumstances. But it's not true. Nowhere in the Bible does it say that. The Bible makes it clear that God will be with you and help you get *through* difficult life experiences. But we live in a broken and sinful world and horrible, devastating events will happen.

However, God has promised that He will not allow you to experience a *temptation* that you cannot handle. With the temptation, there is a way out, so you can bear it. That's good news for us as we daily deal with temptation in our lives.

PRAYER: Praise God for always providing a way out of temptation so that we can resist sin and its entanglements. Thank God for the promises found in His Word that remind us of His power and His faithfulness to us.

NOTES

_____

_____

_____

_____

Spiritual Warfare

TODAY'S TRUTH: All Christians are engaged in a spiritual battle. To walk in victory, we must learn how to stand against the schemes of the enemy.

MAIN SCRIPTURE: Ephesians 6:10-13

As a new Christian, we want you to know some basic truths about what it means to be a Christian. This week we discussed the proactive things you need to do in your walk with Jesus:

- Actively follow Him daily.
- Remain in Him by being connected with Him in a continuing relationship.
- Be in training by practicing spiritual disciplines for the purpose of godliness.
- Be prepared to face temptation to sin.

Finally, we want you to be aware of the reality of spiritual warfare in your life as a new believer.

Before we define and explain what spiritual warfare is, we want you to know that God has equipped you with all that you need before you ever engage in battle. You are to "be strengthened by the Lord and by his vast strength" (Ephesians 6:10). God will make His power available to you for the battle you face. You are not alone, He is with you, and you can tap into His power. God has also provided the equipment necessary for you to use as you experience spiritual warfare. You need to learn how to use the full armor of God and to discipline yourself to put on this armor every day.

How does it make you feel to know that God Himself strengthens us for our spiritual battles? What does this truth reveal about God's desire for our relationship with Him?

_____

_____

Most of us have never experienced military warfare. And all of us are grateful for those who defend our nation and protect our freedoms. Those who have actually been active in the military and in combat better understand the warfare terminology.

Spiritual warfare is defined as the "constant struggle between the flesh and the spirit, between good and evil, between hope and despair, between faith and unbelief, and between carnality and spirituality in a believer. Spiritual warfare is waged on three fronts: personal, corporate, and cosmic. In all three cases the war is waged between unseen enemies, principalities and powers, and evil in high places."[2]

In today's world, we are aware of the unknown realm of warfare, what is not seen but is very real. In the same way that we don't see the tempter when you experience temptation, we can't always see the spiritual battle going on around us.

The different elements of the armor of God are described in Ephesians 6:14-17: "truth like a belt around your waist, righteousness like armor on your chest" (v. 14); peace as sandals for "readiness for the gospel" (v. 15); shield of faith to extinguish "the flaming arrows of the evil one" (v. 16); "helmet of salvation" (v. 17); "sword of the Spirit—which is the word of God" (v. 17).

Consider the kinds of temptations to sin you have experienced this week. Which of the pieces of armor do you need to utilize in order to resist those temptations?

_____

_____

There is a distinction between the first three pieces of armor and the last three. The first three—the belt of truth, the breastplate of righteousness, and the sandals of peace—are pieces of armor you wear all of the time. Much like a baseball player's uniform, you always wear these elements of armor. The other three you "take up," or pick up, to use based on the circumstances.[3] A baseball player picks up his bat or his glove, based on whether he is at bat or on the field. He doesn't use these pieces of equipment all of the time, but as needed depending on his role.

The purpose of the armor of God is to help us resist the enemy and stand firm while we engage in spiritual battle. This conflict requires us to be in a state of readiness at all times. We must put on the armor of God so that we are prepared to resist the enemy.

Have your initial steps of following Christ felt like a spiritual battle to you? If so, how?

_____

_____

PRAYER: Thank God for giving us all we need to stand strong against the enemy's schemes. Depend on God's presence and His strength as you face temptation and challenges this week.

NOTES

_____

_____

Week 4 Journal

Use these pages to journal as you go through the week. If you need guidance, use the following questions to help you.

What truths or promises from God's Word stood out to you this week?

_____

_____

_____

_____

_____

What did you learn about God this week?

_____

_____

_____

_____

_____

How can you obey or apply what you have learned from God's Word this week?

_____

_____

_____

_____

_____

What prayer requests do you have?

_____

_____

_____

_____

_____

_____

_____

_____

_____

_____

_____

_____

_____

_____

_____

_____

_____

_____

_____

_____

_____

I have been crucified with Christ, and I no longer live, but Christ lives in me.
The life I now live in the body, I live by faith in the Son of God, who loved me and
gave himself for me. Galatians 2:20

MY NEW LIFE

Connecting to God's Family

Now as we have many parts in one body, and all the parts do not have the same function, in the same way we who are many are one body in Christ and individually members of one another.

ROMANS 12:4-5

MAIN IDEA:

The church is God's people gathered and sent on God's mission.

WEEK 5

. . .

Christian Community

TODAY'S TRUTH: The church is a community where members relate to one another as God's family.

MAIN SCRIPTURE: Acts 2:42-47

One of the more interesting parts of getting married happens when you begin to blend families together. Your spouse's family will be different from yours in ways that you may not anticipate or expect. Their family has a different rhythm than yours, different traditions, and celebrations. At first this may seem foreign or new, but over time as you begin to settle in, it begins to feel comfortable. When you begin a relationship with Jesus you become a member of the family of God. You are now a son or daughter of God. You are a member of a new global body—the church.

How would you describe or define the church?

_____

_____

While you may have always thought of a church as a building, according to the Bible, the church is not the building but the family of God who meet together *in* the building. In fact, most of the churches in the Bible met in people's homes.

After Jesus ascended into heaven, the Holy Spirit descended as Peter preached on Pentecost. As Peter offered an invitation to follow Jesus, Scripture tell us, "So those who accepted his message were baptized, and that day about three thousand people were added to them" (Acts 2:41). In other words, the people who believed Peter's message became members of the church. Acts 2:42-47 gives us an inside look at the first church. From their example, we can identify several characteristics that should describe Christian community.

The first thing we learn about this new community is that "they devoted themselves to the apostles' teaching" (Acts 2:42). All communities develop around a common cause. For the church, that cause is what Luke called, "the apostles' teaching" (Acts 2:42) or the teachings of Jesus. The central organizing principle of the church is the life-changing message that Jesus died in our place and rose from death in victory over sin so that we may have a free, full, and eternal life. The apostles taught this message and Christian community commits to follow it. This message has been preserved for us in God's Word. We follow the apostles' teaching today when we read the Bible, believe it, and do what it says.

Next, we see they devoted themselves to "fellowship, to the breaking of bread, and to prayer" (Acts 2:42). Fellowship means they had relationships that extended beyond a one-time-a-week meeting. They were devoted to one another. They shared life with one another, ate together, and prayed with and for one another. As this happened, "Everyone was filled with awe, and many wonders and signs were being performed through the apostles" (Acts 2:43).

Awe is not a word that we use much today, but it means reverent fear or worship. As this community of new believers came together, God began to work among them, and their natural response was reverence and appreciation for what God was doing. They saw miracles (wonders and signs) being done by the leaders of the church (see Acts 3 for an example), and it caused them to appreciate the new community they were a part of. Experiencing all this together brought them into deeper relationships with one another. The depth of their relationships was evident in their willingness to sell their possessions to meet the needs of others (Acts 2:45) and eat together daily (Acts 2:46). For them, church was not an event; it was their whole lives. They depended on one another, shared with one another, and sacrificed for one another.

The kind of community these new Christians found was so uncommon and unique that the broader community around them took notice. They were "enjoying the favor of all the people. Every day the Lord added to their number those who were being saved" (Acts 2:47). Their love for God and for each other was visible. The first Christian community became an advertisement for what it means to follow Jesus. At its best, Christian community points the world to the life that can only be found in Jesus.

How have you seen the practices and characteristics of the church found in Acts 2:42-47 displayed in Christian's lives today?

_____

_____

From Acts 2:42-47, we see that God's family is devoted to God's Word, dedicated to each other, committed to meeting needs, and determined to model the gospel to the world so that others can find the same kind of life we've found. As you continue in your new life, you will find that the church is a community—a family—like no other.

Have you found a church family? If not, what has held you back? If so, how has your church family encouraged and poured into you as a new Christian?

_____

_____

PRAYER: Thank God for making you a member of His family. If you don't already have a local church to plug into, ask God for wisdom as you seek one and begin to build relationships with other Christians.

Worship

TODAY'S TRUTH: The church expresses adoration and devotion to God in worship; we worship collectively with other Christians and individually.

MAIN SCRIPTURE: Psalm 96:1-3

We love to celebrate and give time to those things in which we are passionate about! There is also great joy in sharing with others the excitement you experience.

Think about cheering when your favorite sports team comes through with a big win or a great play in a crucial moment. Remember when you told your friends to watch the new show you found on TV or to go read the book you couldn't put down. Think about how excited you were to tell your loved ones about the big news in your life. Why did you do this? No one had to tell you to share your joy because it happened naturally. Your delight produced a response. This experience is natural for you because it is what you were created for. If you are so easily able to celebrate these things, how much more should you be able to celebrate and express joy in God? You were created to worship—to experience joy *in* God and express joy *to* God.

Since God is infinitely good, gracious, and loving, He is more worthy of celebration than anything else in all of creation. The Bible is filled with expressions of worship, particularly in the Book of Psalms. As we read them, we get a great understanding of what it means to worship with our life.

The psalms were songs that the people of Israel wrote to express their heart to God. The author of Psalm 96 invites the whole earth to sing a new song to God: "Sing a new song to the Lord; let the whole earth sing to the Lord" (Psalm 96:1). The word "new" does not mean recently developed. It means fresh. God is so great that we will always be discovering new things about Him. "The whole earth" (Psalm 96:1) will always have a reason to praise Him. The psalmist declared this should happen "day to day" (Psalm 96:2). Just like we read about the Christian community yesterday, worship isn't confined to a single day. Worship isn't just what happens on Sunday; it should happen every single day of your life.

To the psalmist, worship meant proclaiming God's salvation daily, and declaring His glory (His greatness and worth) and His work to anyone who would listen (Psalm 96:2-3). Worship happens when we live with an ever-present recognition of who God is and what He has done for us. When you think about what God has done for you, it should naturally lead you to share your joy and appreciation of God with others. When the Christians in Acts 2:42-47 obeyed the apostles' teaching, pursued community, gave to one another, and showed other people what it meant to know Jesus, they were worshiping. It happened every day to them.

What characteristics of God lead you to worship Him?

_____

_____

_____

The apostle Peter said the church has been saved by God so that "you may proclaim the praises of the one who called you out of darkness and into his marvelous light" (1 Peter 2:9). We respond to God with our whole life because the magnitude of what God has done for us requires such praise. The reason churches all over the world gather on Sundays to sing, listen to preaching, give resources, and seek to make a difference in our world is because we were once lost in darkness. But, because of His great love for us, God rescued us. We have experienced joy in God so we express joy to Him.

We do this every day because the world is filled with people who do not know Jesus. They have not experienced joy in God so they don't know that they should express joy to God. The writer of Psalm 96 and the apostle Peter realized this. Both passages of Scripture urge us to worship God in a way that shows other people who He is so that they can know Him too.

This cannot happen if we only see worship as something that happens once a week through song. Worship happens every day as we commit to glorifying God and enjoying Him forever.

Worship is more than things we do at church like singing songs and praying. What are some practical ways you can worship God in your everyday life?

_____

_____

_____

PRAYER: Praise God today by recounting His qualities that you are grateful for. Thank God for the privilege of glorifying Him each day as you learn more about Him.

NOTES

_____

_____

_____

_____

Preaching / Teaching

TODAY'S TRUTH: The church's teaching builds up followers of Christ.

MAIN SCRIPTURE: Ephesians 4:11-16

Earlier this week we read about the first Christian community, the early church. The first thing we read about them was they "devoted themselves to the apostles' teaching" (Acts 2:42). The apostles walked daily with Jesus during His earthly ministry. They heard Him teach and had the opportunity to ask Him about what He taught. The early church did this because they were the ones who had first-person experience knowing His teachings. A primary responsibility of the church is to continue to share Jesus' teachings. Ephesians 4 explains why the teaching ministry of the church is so important.

Verse 11 says, "And he [Jesus] himself gave some to be apostles, some prophets, some evangelists, some pastors and teachers." This verse simply lists different types of leaders who are involved in the teaching ministry of the church.

Verses 12 tells us why Jesus gave teachers to the church: "equipping the saints for the work of ministry, to build up the body of Christ." Most people assume a pastor's job is to "do ministry stuff." Yet the primary job of teachers in the church, according to Paul, is to train people in the church how to do ministry. This kind of ministry—training others to minister—builds up the body of Christ. "Builds up" means to help grow. Verse 13 shows us the goal of the church's teaching: "until we all reach unity in the faith and in the knowledge of God's Son, growing into maturity with a stature measured by Christ's fullness."

The goal of the church's teaching is to produce fully mature followers of Jesus. Christians should never be stagnant; they should always be growing in their knowledge of and love for God. The early Christians devoted themselves to the apostles' teaching because they were committed to being built up in their faith. Resources like the one you are using right now are made for the purpose of helping people grow in their faith.

What are the characteristics that would describe someone who is growing in faith?

_____

_____

As you grow in your faith, you should commit to becoming a teacher yourself. This doesn't mean you become a full-time minister, but it does mean that you take what you are learning and tell other people. When we love God, we love learning about God and telling other people about what we are learning.

In 2 Timothy 2:2, Paul told Timothy to take what he learned from Paul and teach it to other people who would teach it other people. Do you see the cycle here? The leaders of the church teach, equip, and train the members of the church, who then teach others what they are learning about following Jesus. When this happens we will all "grow in every way into him who is the head—Christ" (Ephesians 4:15). This verse shows us the focus of the church's teaching is Jesus. Ultimately, the teaching of the church should lead us to look like Jesus. The word *Christian* literally means "little Christ." Growing as a Christian means becoming like Christ.

Who has been instrumental in teaching you about Jesus? How has the teaching of God's Word by others helped you grow in your faith?

_____

_____

_____

To be centered in Christ means that He is forever and always the primary focus of the church's message. As we grow in our understanding of what Jesus did for us and the complete transformation that it has brought to our lives, we become more like Jesus and grow in our appreciation of what He has done for us.

The results of the church's teaching are found in verse 16: "From him the whole body, fitted and knit together by every supporting ligament, promotes the growth of the body for building up itself in love by the proper working of each individual part." Here Paul paints a picture of the church coming together in support and unity as a result of a common mission and a common teaching. The church is compared to a body, where each individual member comes together the way muscles, joints, ligaments, and tendons come together to make our physical bodies work. The teaching of the church results in unity that is centered in Christ and committed to telling others about Him.

PRAYER: Spend some time praying for your pastor(s) and others in church leadership. Pray that God would use them to not only point people to Him, but also to teach and train others to do the same. If you are not yet connected in a church family, ask God to help you find one.

NOTES

_____

_____

_____

· · ·

Spiritual Gifts

TODAY'S TRUTH: Every Christ-follower receives spiritual gifts that we are to use to serve one another.

MAIN SCRIPTURE: 1 Corinthians 12:1,4-7

In your life you have probably received gifts. The best gifts are ones we receive just because someone loves us. We don't do anything to earn them and we don't necessarily deserve them, but these gifts are freely given with nothing expected in return. In the Christian life, we talk about grace as a free gift from God. God's grace is not based on anything we have done or our worth before Him. Rather, God's grace is given just because He loves us.

One of the benefits of being a follower of Jesus is that God has given every Christian at least one spiritual gift. Most people have some kind of talent or ability, but only those who have placed their trust in Jesus are the recipients of His incredible spiritual gifts. Every Christian has different God-given gifts to be used to serve others and to build the kingdom of God. Most spiritual gifts are used in the church.

God expects you to recognize, develop, and steward those gifts so that you might fulfill your role in the body, the church. Whatever your spiritual gifts, you are to use them to build up the body of believers. God has gifted you for a specific reason and for a specific task that requires your personal blend of giftedness. You are uniquely designed and gifted!

So, what are some of these gifts? Romans 12:6-8; 1 Corinthians 12:8-10,28-30; Ephesians 4:11; and 1 Peter 4:9-11 contain lists of gifts and roles God has given to the church. God gives a variety of gifts to His people, which is why it is so important that we work together as a body to fulfill His mission. As Christians, we need each other and the various gifts God has given us. Here is a simple definition of these gifts:

- **Leadership:** Aiding the body by leading and directing members to accomplish the goals and purposes of the church.
- **Administration:** Leading the body by steering others to remain on task and organizing according to God-given purposes and long-term goals.
- **Teaching:** Instructing members in the truths of God's Word for the purposes of building up, unifying, and maturing the body.
- **Knowledge:** The God-given ability to learn, know, and explain the precious truths of God's Word.
- **Wisdom:** Discerning the work of the Holy Spirit and applying teachings and actions to the needs of the body.
- **Prophecy:** Proclaiming the Word of God boldly. This builds up the body and leads to conviction of sin.

- **Discernment:** Recognizing the true intentions of people and testing the message and actions of others for the protection and well-being of the body.

- **Exhortation:** Encouraging and motivating other Christians to be involved in and enthusiastic about the work of the Lord.

- **Shepherding:** Looking out for the spiritual welfare of others.

- **Faith:** Trusting God to work beyond the human capabilities of people.

- **Evangelism:** Leading others to Christ effectively and enthusiastically.

- **Missions:** Following God's guidance to plant churches or be missionaries. Moving beyond the church's walls in order to carry out the Great Commission.

- **Service/Helps:** Recognizing the practical needs of people and joyfully giving assistance to meet those needs.

- **Mercy:** Led by compassion to empathize with and serve hurting people.

- **Giving:** Giving freely and joyfully to the work and mission of the body.

- **Hospitality:** The ability to make visitors, guests, and strangers feel at ease.[4]

Do you know what your spiritual gifts are? If so, what are they? How have you used these gifts to serve others?

_____

_____

No matter the gift, all are important and all unite and build up the body of Christ. The same God has given every Christian gifts to use in service to Him. So, you are gifted. If you do not know what your spiritual gifts are, find out today and begin asking God how He might use you and the gifts He has given you as you join Him on mission.

If you are unaware of your spiritual gifts, talk with your pastor about taking a recommended spiritual gifts assessment in your church, or go to LifeWay.com/SpiritualGiftsInventory. Look to the leadership at your church to help you identify your gifts and the opportunities that are available for you to serve.

How do spiritual gifts help us understand the value and worth of every member of the body?

_____

_____

PRAYER: Ask God to help you identify, understand, and use the gifts He has graciously given you to accomplish His mission.

Baptism and the Lord's Supper

TODAY'S TRUTH: The church has two practices modeled and taught by Jesus: believer's baptism and the Lord's Supper.

MAIN SCRIPTURE: Matthew 28:19-20; 1 Corinthians 11:23-26

The imagery the Bible uses to describe the church helps us understand what it means to be the church. This week, we have seen that the church is the family of God. The Bible also calls the church the "bride of Christ" (Ephesians 5:22-33). The image of marriage is particularly helpful in understanding baptism and the Lord's Supper.

During His earthly ministry, Jesus modeled and taught (or ordained, which is where we get the word "ordinances") these two practices given to the church to shape it. These ordinances help us remember and rehearse what God has accomplished on our behalf through the gospel. Let's look at each one individually.

Baptism is the immersion of a believer in water in the name of the Father, the Son, and the Holy Spirit. Jesus modeled baptism for us when He was baptized by John the Baptist in the Jordan River (Matthew 3:13-17). He commanded His disciples to baptize new followers of Him in the Great Commission (Matthew 28:18-20). When a Christian follows Jesus' example and obeys His command to be baptized they are saying to the church and to the whole world, "I am a follower of Jesus. I am dead to sin and alive to Christ." Going under the water symbolizes Christ's death; coming back up out of the water symbolizes His resurrection. Baptism demonstrates our initial identification with Christ and His church.

To come back to the wedding image the Bible uses, baptism can be similar to wearing a wedding ring. A ring is the initial symbol a husband and wife gives to each other to symbolize their union. It demonstrates to the world, and before God, that this man and this woman are committed to one another in a marriage. Putting the ring on or taking it off does not make a person more or less married. Rather, it is an important symbol communicating a deeper reality.

Similarly, baptism does not make someone a Christian. The water and the words have no unique power to save. Since the person being baptized is already a follower of Jesus, baptism is an outward demonstration of what has already taken place inside a person's soul. Baptism allows us to affirm and celebrate together the Lord's grace and power to save.

Have you been baptized? If not, what is hindering you from doing so? If you have, describe the joy that came with sharing your new life in Jesus with others.

_____

_____

_____

The Lord's Supper (also known as communion) is the second symbol or ordinance of the church. This practice is rooted in the final meal Jesus had with His disciples before He went to the cross (read Paul's words in 1 Corinthians 11:23-26). When we engage in the Lord's Supper, we remember what Jesus did and reflect upon the day when He will return. The Lord's Supper celebrates our continual identification with Christ and His church.

If baptism is like a wedding ring, we can think of the Lord's Supper like an anniversary. A good marriage is filled with times when the husband and wife stop and reflect upon their relationship and celebrate the gift God has given them in each other. However, these feelings are particularly heightened on an anniversary. This is a day to look back on and celebrate the marriage, while expressing hope for the future. The couple commits to one another anew and thanks God for what He has done.

While we celebrate the Lord's Supper much more frequently than a wedding anniversary, this practice was given to the church to continually remember what Jesus has done. Taking the bread and the cup provide an opportunity for the church to come together and remember God's enduring faithfulness.

What are some benefits of remembering and celebrating what Jesus has done?

_____

_____

_____

Baptism and the Lord's Supper are the means Christ has ordained to celebrate and reflect upon His work in our lives and through the church. As the church celebrates baptism and partakes of the Lord's Supper, they are shaped further into the image and likeness of Jesus. Through them we experience the goodness of Jesus and grow in our relationship with Him.

PRAYER: Thank God for the ordinances of baptism and the Lord's Supper and the opportunities you have to worship through and celebrate them with other Christians. Ask God to use these ordinances to spur you to remember Him in all that you do.

Week 5 Journal

Use these pages to journal as you go through the week. If you need guidance, use the following questions to help you.

What truths or promises from God's Word stood out to you this week?

_____

_____

_____

_____

_____

What did you learn about God this week?

_____

_____

_____

_____

_____

How can you obey or apply what you have learned from God's Word this week?

_____

_____

_____

_____

_____

What prayer requests do you have?

_____

_____

_____

_____

_____

_____

_____

_____

_____

_____

_____

_____

_____

_____

_____

_____

_____

_____

_____

_____

Joining God on Mission

Go, therefore, and make disciples of all nations, baptizing them in the name of the Father and of the Son and of the Holy Spirit, teaching them to observe everything I have commanded you. And remember, I am with you always, to the end of the age.

MATTHEW 28:19-20

MAIN IDEA:

God's will for Christians is that we glorify God and make Him known to the world.

• • •

MY NEW LIFE

Joining God in His Mission

TODAY'S TRUTH: We are called to live our lives on mission with the good news of Jesus.

MAIN SCRIPTURE: John 20:21

Reflect on the word "mission" for a few moments. What comes to mind?

Perhaps you thought of a mission statement for a company or another organization—a statement of purpose that guides employees or members as they make choices to grow. Possibly you thought of an action movie in which agents are tasked with achieving near hopeless goals and, therefore, have the opportunity to accept or reject that mission. If you have been involved in a church, the idea of a "mission trip" came to mind. A mission trip usually takes the form of traveling to a distant (sometimes foreign) location in order to help people in need and share Jesus with them.

Take an honest assessment of how you spend your time, money, and other resources. What would you say is your life's mission? What would those with whom you do life with say is your life's mission?

_____

_____

_____

It's important to understand the different nuances or uses of the word "mission" because followers of Jesus live on mission with the good news of Jesus Christ. But what exactly does that mean?

In the Gospel of John, we find a short passage that features Jesus' own words to His disciples about their mission: "When it was evening of that first day of the week, the disciples were gathered together with the doors locked because they feared the Jews. Jesus came, stood among them, and said to them, 'Peace be with you.' Having said this, he showed them his hands and his side. So, the disciples rejoiced when they saw the Lord. Jesus said to them again, 'Peace be with you. As the Father has sent me, I also send you'" (John 20:19-21).

The events described in this passage take place near the end of the day on which Jesus was resurrected. Some of Jesus' disciples were huddled up in a home behind locked doors, fearful for their lives. They thought Jesus was dead. What did the future hold for them? It was at that moment that Jesus came to them, speaking peace into their lives and telling them that they have a mission, summed up in verse 21: "Peace be with you. As the Father has sent me, I also send you."

Knowing this context, there are a couple of things you can discern about what it means to live on mission as a disciple of Jesus.

First, don't miss the fact that the first followers of Jesus needed to be told that they had a mission. One moment the disciples hid behind lock doors, fearful in the wake of Jesus' death, and afraid that the Jews would come for them to imprison them or worse. The next moment they are at peace, empowered to share the good news of Jesus with others. Being on mission for Jesus did not come naturally or even logically to them. Jesus' resurrection and instruction brought clarity to the disciples as to what their purpose would be, and it does the same for you. Your mission is to tell others about Jesus.

What fears do you need to overcome, knowing that Jesus is resurrected and desires to use you to accomplish His mission?

_____

_____

_____

Second, by twice stating, "Peace be with you" (John 20:19,21), it's clear that your mission is not to be understood as a harsh assignment given by a heartless, tyrannical God who is unconcerned about your welfare and cares only that we fulfill this mission. Quite the opposite. God is for you. He wants you to experience the peace that He accomplished for you through the life, death, and resurrection of His Son, Jesus. His love and care for you is not based on your ability to fulfill your new mission, but on Jesus' fulfillment of His!

Jesus clearly wants you to rest in the fact that in the same way He was successful in His mission (as evidenced by His resurrection), you will be successful in yours of telling the world about Him. In fact, it's only because Jesus accomplished His mission that you will accomplish yours. Becoming a follower of Jesus and joining His mission is similar to being chosen for the team that you know for certain will win the world championship. Knowing this gives you confidence to press on through the ups and downs.

You can step confidently into any opportunity to tell someone about Jesus. Why? Because Jesus has risen from the dead, is in heaven currently, and will one day come back to bring His people into His kingdom where we will be in His presence for eternity. You will join God in His mission because Jesus is coming back!

PRAYER: Pray that you would live a life sold out for Jesus' mission. As you pray, look above at the list of fears you wrote. Ask God to help you overcome those fears and to give you confidence in Him as He works in and through you to accomplish His mission.

Evangelism

TODAY'S TRUTH: We are commanded to be God's witnesses by sharing the gospel so that all may hear the good news of Jesus Christ.

MAIN SCRIPTURE: Acts 1:8

Few things are more valuable for getting to the truth of something that may have happened than a witness—someone who can testify to the truthfulness of something because he or she personally saw what happened. If no other evidence exists to help one come to a conclusion, having one or more witnesses to the event go a long way in helping determine what took place.

In 1 Corinthians 15:6, the apostle Paul mentions that Jesus appeared to more than five hundred people after His resurrection. Think of it: more than five hundred witnesses saw first hand the risen Jesus Christ! How might that stand up in a court of law?

As a new believer, you obviously did not physically see a risen Jesus; but since the moment you were saved, you have perceived that what the Bible says about Jesus is true. Jesus is the Son of God who came in the flesh, lived the sinless life you could not live, died on the cross to take the judgment of God that you deserve, and then overcame the penalty of death on your behalf through His resurrection. Because you believe this to be true, you are now a witness of that truth to others.

This has been the case for all believers since Jesus' resurrection and ascension. Let's take a look at Acts 1:8: "But you will receive power when the Holy Spirit has come on you, and you will be my witnesses in Jerusalem, in all Judea and Samaria, and to the end of the earth."

What did Jesus promise His disciples in Acts 1:8?
What command did He then give them?

_____

_____

_____

It's fascinating that Jesus' followers, seeing His power, wondered if He would use it. Jesus responded that it was His witnesses that would have power. Not power to establish a political kingdom, but power to be effective witnesses about Jesus (His teachings, life, death, and resurrection). That power would come in the form of the person—the Holy Spirit.

Why was the coming of the Holy Spirit essential to the disciples' being witnesses? Why is this important for you today as you seek to share the good news of Jesus with others?

_____

_____

_____

Jesus connected the power to accomplish the mission He was giving to His followers with the presence of the Holy Spirit. Jesus' disciples were to rely upon the power of the Holy Spirit to share the truth of the gospel locally and globally. The Spirit enables you to overcome your fears and to fulfill what Jesus has asked you to do as a witness for Him.

It is important to notice that power _from_ God is essential for you to be a witness _for_ God. The world is inundated with obstacles to the truthfulness of your witness. Only the Holy Spirit can open the eyes and hearts of those to whom you witness in order to make a difference in their lives. It is also important to notice that the call to witness was not limited to any select group of people; it spread from the apostles to the 120 believers, and further, per the references in the Book of Acts. Nor can we restrict this call only to some kind of "professional ministry." Every believer should be a witness; every believer should be able to function for the Savior from the other side of the street to the other side of the world.

What was your life like before Jesus? How did you come to know Him? How is your life now different because of Jesus? Write these answers out in detail on another sheet of paper in preparation to share this good news of what Jesus has done in your heart.

_____

_____

With whom can you share your story? What steps will you take to do this?

_____

_____

_____

PRAYER: Praise God for making you one of His own. Thank Him for the special privilege He has given you to represent Him. Ask God to give you confidence in Him, words to speak, and the opportunities to speak them with those who do not yet know Him.

Giving / Tithing

TODAY'S TRUTH: We respond to God's goodness by giving a tithe of our income.

MAIN SCRIPTURE: 2 Corinthians 9:7; Malachi 3:7-10

Jesus Christ is Lord is the most basic statement of faith for the new believer. The lordship of Jesus covers every aspect of our lives. In week one, day 3, we introduced the meaning of the word "Lord." The word *Lord* means "master" or "boss." The idea that Jesus is Lord means He is in charge, He is in control, and He calls the shots. Your response to His lordship is to obey Him, and to say yes to Him when He speaks to you through His Word. It means that you know His teachings and follow them. When you experience tension between what you desire to do and what Jesus says you should do, you yield to Him.

Jesus' lordship includes your money and possessions. This may be a new concept for you as a new Christian. Jesus is Lord over your money and possessions.

Here's the biblical perspective on money and possessions:

- God owns everything. Everything belongs to Him.

- All that we possess has been given to us by God.

- He entrusts what He owns to us. We are stewards of what belongs to Him.

So, everything in your possession belongs to God. It isn't yours. Nothing you have—your money, your stuff, your relationships, your time—is yours. It is all God's. All that you have God graciously gave to you. Because God is the owner, you are merely a steward, a manager of God's resources. This new perspective changes everything.

This leads us to the topic of giving, which includes tithes or offerings. Giving is a very sensitive topic. It's personal. But God, who has graciously given you all that you possess and who gave His only Son for us, calls us to give cheerfully, generously, and faithfully. As Christians, we do this as an act of worship; we give to Him who owns it all as an act of obedience to the One who commands us to give.

How have you viewed your money and material possessions in the past?

_____

_____

_____

Many who do not know God make money and possessions their God. The world's approach is to accumulate material wealth to ensure a pleasant and enjoyable life of ease. But the Christian knows the truth that everything is God's and they can live under the knowledge that "it was never mine to begin with." What an incredibly freeing place to be! As Christians, we are able to bring glory to God by giving what is His to help further His kingdom. He intends that we use material blessings unselfishly to minister to others.

So, what does giving back to God look like? First and foremost, it's giving back to His church. In Malachi 3:7-10, God spoke through this prophet to tell the Israelites to turn their hearts back to Him. They had lost focus and were no longer following the Lord. So God offered the Israelites an opportunity to repent and to receive His blessings. The Lord pointed to a particular way the people should return to Him—they needed to stop robbing Him. The Old Testament clearly taught the people were to bring a tenth of their income from their produce and flocks to the temple as an offering to God. The Hebrew word translated *tithe* literally means "a tenth."

The practice of giving a tithe to the Lord isn't just for Old Testament believers. Today, giving a tithe of your income to God accomplishes two things. The purpose of tithing is to bring the giver into a closer relationship with God. Giving demonstrates several important aspects of our relationship with God. It is an act of obedience and an expression of devotion to the Lord. It acknowledges that God owns everything and that we are merely stewards of what He has entrusted to us. It also expresses faith in God as our Provider, trusting Him to meet our needs with what remains. To fail to give is to miss His blessings found in the joy of giving. From a practical perspective, God's people giving financially to the church provides support for ministers and its ministries.

Have you started to give to your church? Do you know that your generosity not only keeps the church going but it also reveals your love for Christ, helps the body of Christ, and gives to the work of Christ? Your giving as an act of worship is furthering God's kingdom by providing ministry opportunities.

You may be thinking to yourself, "But I don't have a lot to give." God is not interested in the amount given; rather, it's all about the heart in which the giver gives. Luke 21:1-4 says Jesus "looked up and saw the rich dropping their offerings into the temple treasury. He also saw a poor widow dropping in two tiny coins. 'Truly I tell you,' he said, 'this poor widow has put in more than all of them. For all these people have put in gifts out of their surplus, but she out of her poverty has put in all she had to live on.'"

What obstacles might prevent you from giving a tithe or giving cheerfully?
Record your responses and then ask God in prayer to remove these hindrances.

_____

_____

PRAYER: Thank God for His generosity toward you. Invite Him to grow you in your obedience and generosity toward Him in regard to your finances. Ask Him to give you wisdom for what He wants you to give and where He wants you to give.

Sacrifice

TODAY'S TRUTH: Our response as Christ-followers is to offer our lives to God in all we do.

MAIN SCRIPTURE: Romans 12:1-2

Love always requires a sacrifice. Whether it's a sacrifice of time, priorities, or our own desires, love means that we set aside the things we value to give of ourselves to others. No matter the relationship, we're called to a sacrificial love.

Nowhere is this reality more clear than on the cross, where Jesus gave His own life to bring us peace with God, where God gave His precious Son for our benefit. The cross is the greatest picture of sacrifice the world has ever seen, and it is also the greatest example of love the world has ever known. Living in light of Christ's sacrifice causes us to lay aside our priorities and goals to pursue the upward call of Christ. The gospel motivates us to give our whole lives as a sacrifice to God.

Now, let's be honest here. We live in a society that screams "me first." We're told to be whoever we want to be, to do whatever feels good, and to find our happiness by whatever means necessary. We are surrounded by the shouts of "me first." It can be difficult to live a life of sacrifice that is holy and pleasing to God. Paul said in Romans 12:1: "Therefore, brothers and sisters, in view of the mercies of God, I urge you to present your bodies as a living sacrifice, holy and pleasing to God; this is your true worship." Let's acknowledge that because of our surrounding culture, living a life of sacrifice isn't easy. However, it is worth it!

What evidence can people see that God has transformed you?

_____

_____

_____

The transformation of our mind isn't a call to make this change on our own; it's the Holy Spirit doing this work in and through us. On our end, though, it's a daily surrender to His will. This act of worship is saying, "God, this life is Yours. My family, my relationships, my finances, my work, my everything—it's all Yours." What we are offering to God is what we do, the way we act, and the way we live. As Christians, we are to fully sacrifice, or hand over control of, our lives to God.

What have you found to be the most difficult thing in offering your life to God? What has been the best thing about your decision to give your life over to God?

_____

_____

_____

So what does this look like in our everyday lives? In marriage, it's not about getting anything, but giving to and serving your spouse. In parenting, it's not about raising children that fit in the box of who you would like for them to become; rather, it's raising children in the Lord and pointing them to Jesus each step of the way. It's desiring God's will for their lives instead of your own selfish longings for them. With your finances, it's acknowledging that your money is God's. He is the good Giver of it, and it is His. So how do you best steward it to honor Him? In your job it's a transition in thinking, "I have to do this and I just want to go in, be done, and go home," to "I get to work hard to God's glory today!" There are so many other areas of our lives in which we lay down the wants and desires that our world tells us we need, in order to say, "God, this life is Yours and I want to honor and glorify You with it."

Now that you are a Christian, your daily response should be living for Him and seeking His Word for continual heart change. You are called to give your life to God as you refuse to be conformed to the world and its values any longer. How do we daily refuse to conform to the world and choose to be transformed? Stay in His Word. You need not wander aimlessly through life searching for God's will. His will for your life is wrapped up in His Word. As you seek God, He will give you a greater understanding of His will.

God's words are strong and powerful, and He has given them to you in the Bible. Read God's Word. Know His Word. Be changed by His Word. As you do, offer your life to Him as a daily response.

PRAYER: Pray that God would empower you to live your life as a living sacrifice to Him through the transformation of your mind. Pray that you would be transformed by His Word and reject conformity to the world. Ask for wisdom to better understand God's will as your life is transformed and dedicated to Him.

NOTES

_____

_____

_____

_____

Holiness

TODAY'S TRUTH: Christians are set apart for God's purposes.

MAIN SCRIPTURE: Leviticus 11:45

When we think of a calling, we typically consider what someone does with his or her life vocationally. Many would go so far as to say that their calling is what they live for or what they were made for. It might be a passion they have or work that brings great fulfillment. However, to understand that our calling goes beyond our vocation is incredibly important for our Christian walk. We, as Christians, have been called to do much more!

As Christians, we are called to live in ways that honor God and demonstrate our love toward Him and others. By doing this, we are set apart from a world that does not live to love and honor God. This being set apart or unique in the world we live in is known as holiness. God has called you to this. Oftentimes, when we hear the word "holiness," we think of moral purity. That is correct in that holiness means we are to live as Christ, who is holy and unblemished. We do this to honor and obey God. However, holiness also means that God has set us apart for His mission and purposes.

How do you see yourself as different from the world as a result of your faith in Jesus?

_____

_____

_____

_____

You are called to be a holy person as a Christian. You are called to live your life differently than the "old you" and that of the world around you. You are called to no longer position yourself to live for your own personal goals and wishes, but to instead position yourself to serve God and live for Him. When you do this, you're asking God to use you for His purposes because He is holy and worthy of all that you have to give. What the Lord said to the Israelites in Leviticus 11:45 is as true for you as it was for them: "you must be holy because I am holy."

It's important to note that we don't just become holy on our own. Holiness isn't something we can attain through our own effort; rather, it is the work of God. When we recognize who Jesus is and what He has done, we will desire to become more and more like Him. He is faithful to continually change our heart to become like His. This is called *sanctification*. Sanctification is the process of the Christian becoming more and more like Jesus while living on this earth. It is the actual growth in holiness that the Holy Spirit does in the life of the Christian.

As you become more and more like Christ, He will give you His heart, His eyes, His ears, His words, His compassion, His grace, and His love for all people. Because of Jesus, your heart has been changed. You have been set apart in a way that when you allow yourself to be used by Him, the Holy Spirit will work in and through you to fulfill His purposes.

In what ways has God made you more like Himself and in what ways has your thinking changed?

_____

_____

_____

So, what does living a life set apart for God's purposes look like? You are holy because as a Christian, you now have the Holy Spirit. Because Christians are God's children and have the indwelling of the Holy Spirit, we are to live as God's representatives on earth. Christians are called to live lives of holiness and persuasion, proclaiming the gospel of Jesus. We are to live as those who love God, who have been redeemed, transformed, and given hope in Jesus. Because of this new life in Jesus, your circumstances, your old life, and the world around you cannot get a foothold. You are changed from the inside out and you have been called to live differently in order to be used by God for His purposes.

In what ways do you need to live for His purposes that you have not done in the past? How might doing this point those around you to Jesus?

_____

_____

_____

PRAYER: Thank God for redeeming you and allowing you to live a life that is filled with hope because of your new relationship with Him. Pray that as you live, you would do so on mission, and that those around you would be transformed by the Holy Spirit, who is working in and through you.

NOTES

_____

_____

_____

_____

Week 6 Journal

Use these pages to journal as you go through the week. If you need guidance, use the following questions to help you.

What truths or promises from God's Word stood out to you this week?

_____

_____

_____

_____

_____

What did you learn about God this week?

_____

_____

_____

_____

_____

How can you obey or apply what you have learned from God's Word this week?

_____

_____

_____

_____

_____

What prayer requests do you have?

_____

_____

_____

_____

_____

_____

_____

_____

_____

_____

_____

_____

_____

_____

_____

_____

_____

WEEKLY TRUTH TO MEMORIZE:

**Go, therefore, and make disciples of all nations, baptizing them in
the name of the Father and of the Son and of the Holy Spirit, teaching them to
observe everything I have commanded you. And remember, I am with you always,
to the end of the age. Matthew 28:19-20**

MY NEW LIFE

Next Steps

You did it! So, what now? We hope that in the time you have spent in this book, you have grown in your trust in Jesus, gotten plugged into a church family, and connected in deep relationships with other Christians. If you have not, it's not too late! If you are looking for another resource to help you grow in your faith, you'll find the types of books and resources you are looking for at LifeWay.com.

As you continue on in your faith journey, we encourage you to simply keep going.

- Continue to read God's Word and pray often. If you need a scheduled plan on where to start reading Scripture, see the Bible reading plan on page 96.

- If you haven't already done so, get plugged into a Bible study group. Allow mature Christians to pour into you, teach you, and encourage you in your faith journey.

- Continue to make Jesus central in your life and seek after Him each day. Allow the Holy Spirit to work in and through you, making you more and more like Jesus.

- And, continue to trust Him. That's not always easy, as we have so many things in this world fighting for our trust, time, and focus. Trust in His love for you, His goodness, His faithfulness, and His grace. He is always trustworthy!

You may have already noticed that being a Christian doesn't mean life gets any easier. It's much better because of the hope you have in Jesus, but that doesn't mean difficult circumstances won't come your way. Grab hold of Jesus' words here as you endure difficulty:

> **"I have told you these things so that in me you may have peace.**
> **You will have suffering in this world. Be courageous!**
> **I have conquered the world"** (John 16:33).

This is a simple call to trust Him. Jesus has died for you, was raised to life for you, and is coming back for you. He has conquered sin and death, and so, no matter what difficulty we face, we always know we have the victory through Jesus. No matter what hardship you are up against, you have Jesus now and for eternity. That is a joy that can never be taken away.

What an amazing God we serve. We are so thankful to know that you have placed your trust in Jesus and we are praying for you. Be encouraged by this prayer and pray it for yourself and other Christians you know.

> **"For this reason also, since the day we heard this, we haven't stopped praying for you. We are asking that you may be filled with the knowledge of his will in all wisdom and spiritual understanding, so that you may walk worthy of the Lord, fully pleasing to him: bearing fruit in every good work and growing in the knowledge of God, being strengthened with all power, according to his glorious might, so that you may have great endurance and patience, joyfully giving thanks to the Father, who has enabled you to share in the saints' inheritance in the light. He has rescued us from the domain of darkness and transferred us into the kingdom of the Son he loves. In him we have redemption, the forgiveness of sins"** (Colossians 1:9-14).

Now, as Jesus has called you to do: Go and make disciples, and remember that He is with you every step of the way!

ENDNOTES

1. Dallas Willard, *The Spirit of the Disciplines: Understanding How God Changes Lives* (HarperOne: New York), 158.
2. *Nelson's New Christian Dictionary: The Authoritative Resource on the Christian World* (Thomas Nelson: Nashville), 719.
3. Tony Evans, *Victory In Spiritual Warfare: Field Guide for Battle* (B&H Publishing: Nashville) 29.
4. Adapted from https://s3.amazonaws.com/lifewayblogs/wp-content/uploads/sites/83/2018/03/21175431/DOC-Spiritual-Gifts-List-2.pdf.

Bible Reading Plan

ONE-MONTH READING PLAN THROUGH THE BOOK OF JOHN

☐ 1:1-28

☐ 1:29-51

☐ 2:1-25

☐ 3:1-21

☐ 3:22-36

☐ 4:1-26

☐ 4:27-54

☐ 5:1-16

☐ 5:17-47

☐ 6:1-21

☐ 6:22-71

☐ 7:1-24

☐ 7:25-53

☐ 8:1-20

☐ 8:21-59

☐ 9:1-41

☐ 10:1-30

☐ 10:31-42

☐ 11:1-27

☐ 11:28-57

☐ 12:1-19

☐ 13:1-38

☐ 14:1-31

☐ 15:1-27

☐ 16:1-33

☐ 17:1-26

☐ 18:1-40

☐ 19:1-16

☐ 19:17-42

☐ 20:1-31

☐ 21:1-25